THE UNIVERSITY OF MICHIGAN
CENTER FOR CHINESE STUDIES

MICHIGAN PAPERS IN CHINESE STUDIES
No. 16

AN ANNOTATED BIBLIOGRAPHY
of
CHINESE PAINTING CATALOGUES AND RELATED TEXTS

Hin-cheung Lovell
Freer Gallery of Art
Smithsonian Institution

Ann Arbor

Center for Chinese Studies
The University of Michigan

1973

Open access edition funded by the National Endowment for the Humanities/ Andrew W. Mellon Foundation Humanities Open Book Program.

Copyright © 1973

by

Center for Chinese Studies
The University of Michigan

ISBN 978-0-89264-016-4 (hardcover)
ISBN 978-0-472-03840-4 (paper)
ISBN 978-0-472-12821-1 (ebook)
ISBN 978-0-472-90221-7 (open access)

The text of this book is licensed under a Creative Commons Attribution-NonCommercial-NoDerivatives 4.0 International License: https://creativecommons.org/licenses/by-nc-nd/4.0/

Table of Contents

Preface..i

List of Abbreviations............................v

ANNOTATED BIBLIOGRAPHY of the 108 titles in
 John C. Ferguson's Li-tai chu-lu hua mu.......1

ANNOTATED BIBLIOGRAPHY of 22 additional
 titles.......................................99

Index of Names................................125

Index of Titles...............................133

Preface

The student of Chinese painting who is at all concerned with its textual aspects must from time to time consult John C. Ferguson's Li-tai chu-lu hua mu 歷代著錄畫目 (Peking, 1934; reprint: Taipei, 1968), an index to Chinese paintings recorded in Chinese catalogues. Having consulted Ferguson, he is certain to want to know more about the catalogues in which the paintings are recorded: their compilers, the date of their compilation, their scope, their derivation, their merits and shortcomings, and so on.

This Annotated Bibliography of Chinese Painting Catalogues and Related Texts grew out of notes I had been making for my own reference since 1969. It occurred to me that there might be a need for an annotated bibliography in English among students whose knowledge of Chinese is not proficient enough for them to consult the annotated bibliographies which exist in Chinese, principally Shu hua shu-lu chieh-t'i 書畫書錄解題 by Yü Shao-sung 余紹宋 (Peking, 1932; reprint: Taipei, 1968), and Ssu-pu tsung-lu i-shu pien 四部總錄藝術編 by Ting Fu-pao 丁福保 and Chou Yün-ch'ing 周雲青 (Shanghai, 1957). To those who have no difficulty with the language, the bibliography may be a tool providing the basic information on the catalogues in an easily available form.

Essentially, then, the Annotated Bibliography is a companion to Ferguson, and as such, it consists of a review of each of the 108 titles used by him in Li-tai chu-lu hua mu as given in his bibliography. The reviews are arranged as far as possible in a chronological order according to the date of compilation. They are numbered consecutively from "1" to "108".

The heading at the beginning of each entry gives the following information:
(a) The name of the compiler.
(b) The title of the text.
(c) Whenever possible, the date of compilation. This information is usually in the author's preface or someone else's preface. If no such information is available, an approximate date will be given in the entry, and the date of the compiler's death will determine the position of the review.
(d) The number of chüan in the text.
(e) In parentheses, a cross-reference to the numbering system used in Ferguson's bibliography. For example, in my first entry, (Ferguson, 9, 12) indicates that the text Chen-kuan kung ssu hua shih is listed in Ferguson's bibliography as the twelfth title under the nine-stroke group because the first character chen has nine strokes.
(f) Citation of the most recent, most easily accessible and least expensive edition or editions. In many cases, this means the editions in Mei-shu ts'ung-shu and I-shu ts'ung-pien, or the most recent facsimile reprints in the I-shu shang-chien hsüan-chen series produced in Taipei. These publications are readily available and inexpensive enough to be within the reach of the serious student and certainly of those universities where the study of Chinese art is a recently established discipline. The student who

feels inclined to explore the problem of textual variations in different editions can do so on his own initiative. In the small number of instances where the rule of citing a recent edition or reprint is not feasible, the citation is to the particular edition I used.

(g) In the cases of those titles not included in Mei-shu ts'ung-shu, I-shu ts'ung-pien, I-shu shang-chien hsüan-chen, or excerpted in P'ei-wen-chai shu hua p'u, the name of the institution given in square brackets indicates the source of the text consulted.

In addition to the reviews of the 108 titles used by Ferguson, there is a supplement of reviews of twenty-two other texts not used by him but which are pertinent to our purpose. Some of these were compiled after 1934 and others were simply not used by him either because they were unavailable or unknown to him. These reviews, bearing numbers "S.1" to "S.22", are also arranged chronologically and are given the same treatment as the other 108 titles. This list of twenty-two is by no means an exhaustive one of the texts omitted by Ferguson, but it does include some obvious and frequently encountered titles.

It is impossible in a work of this nature to subject each text to the kind of intensive study carried out, for example, by Professor Soper on Kuo Jo-hsü's T'u-hua chien-wen chih. In my reviews, I have tended to devote greater space to the more important texts, and to be especially severe in my criticism of the more pretentious compilations.

Although I tried to arrive at my own assessment of each text, <u>Shu hua shu-lu chieh-t'i</u> and <u>Ssu-pu tsung-lu i-shu pien</u> were inevitably much consulted. I would like to express my appreciation of the assistance of Dr. K.T. Wu and his staff of the Orientalia Division, Library of Congress; of Miss Jean Finch of the Stanford University Art Library; of the Harvard-Yenching Institute Library; and of the University of Chicago Library. A number of elusive texts were located with the help of Sewell Oertling, Celia Riely, Lothar Ledderose, and Marilyn Fu. Mr. Wang Nan-p'ing supplied the dates of two modern collectors. The manuscript was read by Mr. Wan Wei-ying, Head of the Asia Library, University of Michigan, who made a number of suggestions for improvement. Bibliographical problems were solved with the help of Celia Hu, Assistant Librarian at the Freer Gallery; she also had the onerous task of checking two typescripts. Throughout the preparation of the <u>Annotated Bibliography</u>, Thomas Lawton was of assistance in ways too numerous to record; to him I owe a special debt. But for his repeated assurances that the project was worth finishing, I would surely have at some exasperated moment consigned the half-typed script to the Potomac.

Hin-cheung Lovell
Freer Gallery of Art
September, 1973

List of Abbreviations

CPTSTS   Chih-pu-tsu-chai ts'ung-shu 知不足齋叢書. (Compiled by Pao T'ing-po 鮑廷博; preface dated 1776. 1882 edition).

CSSHSP   Chang shih shu hua ssu piao 張氏書畫四表. (1908 edition).

GMS   Gunnar Martins Samling av Kinesisk och Japansk Litteratur. (Stockholm, 1947).

HFLPC   Han-fen-lou pi-chi 涵芬樓秘笈. (Compiled 1916-26).

HH   Han hai 函海. (Compiled by Li Tiao-yüan 李調元; preface dated 1782. 1882 edition).

ISSCHC   I-shu shang-chien hsüan-chen 藝術賞鑑選珍. (Han-hua 漢華 Co., Taipei, Series I-V and continuing, 1970-).

ISTP   I-shu ts'ung-pien 藝術叢編. (Compiled by Yang Chia-lo 楊家駱, Taipei, preface 1962).

KHCPWK   Kuo-hsüeh chen-pen wen-k'u 國學珍本文庫. (Shanghai, 1935-36).

MTISCWCHK Ming-tai i-shu-chia wen-chi hui-k'an 明代藝術家文集彙刊. (Taipei, 1968).

MSTS	Mei-shu ts'ung-shu 美術叢書. (Compiled by Teng Shih 鄧實 and Huang Pin-hung 黃賓虹, 1912-36. Reprint of the 1947 enlarged edition, Taipei, n.d.).
PWCSHP	P'ei-wen-chai shu hua p'u 佩文齋書畫譜. (Compiled 1708). See entry 51.
SKCS	Ssu-k'u ch'üan-shu 四庫全書. ("Complete Library in Four Branches of Literature", compiled by order of the Ch'ien-lung emperor, 1773-85).
SHCSTMTY	Ssu-k'u ch'üan-shu tsung-mu t'i-yao 四庫全書總目提要. (Reviews of the 3,450 titles included in, and the 6,780 titles excluded from, SKCS, 1781).
SLTS	Sung-lin ts'ung-shu 松鄰叢書. (Compiled by Wu Ch'ang-shou 吳昌綬, 1917-18).
TSCC	Ts'ung-shu chi-ch'eng 叢書集成. (Commercial Press, Shanghai, 1935-37).
WSSHY	Wang shih shu hua yüan 王氏書畫苑. (Compiled by Wang Shih-chen 王世貞 [died 1590] with supplement compiled by Chan Ching-feng 詹景鳳 in 1590; 1922 edition).

1. P'ei Hsiao-yüan 裴孝源, Chen-kuan kung ssu hua shih 貞觀公私畫史. Preface dated 639. 1 chüan. (Ferguson, 9, 12). MSTS, vol. 7, II/3, and ISTP, vol. 8, no. 57, both based on SKCS.

Little is known about P'ei Hsiao-yüan except that he lived in the first half of the seventh century and that his official title was Chung-shu she-jen 中書舍人 (Drafting Official of the Secretariat). The "Chen-kuan" in the title of the text refers to the fact that it was compiled sometime during that reign, 627-650 A.D. In the SKCS text, there is a preface dated the thirteenth year of Chen-kuan, corresponding to 639 A.D. The dated preface is not included in either the MSTS or the ISTP edition, but is referred to in the SKCSTMTY review which appears in both.

Chen-kuan kung ssu hua shih is the earliest extant catalogue of paintings. It comprises the titles of 293 paintings, 281 of which are grouped under 53 artists, and 12 are anonymous. They range from Chin 晉 to T'ang. Following this is a list of 47 temples in different cities with frescoes by known artists. The vast majority of the 293 paintings were from the Sui imperial collection.

Although there is very little information apart from the titles of the paintings, what little there is is of considerable interest. In a few instances, some imperial seals and colophons are noted. Under Lu T'an-wei 陸探微, there are two groups of paintings, one of which P'ei considered genuine, the other he considered doubtful despite their traditional attri-

1

bution. Therein lies the first attempt at authentication in extant painting catalogues.

For a discussion of the problems of this text, see the review in SKCSTMTY as given in MSTS and ISTP.

2. Kuo Jo-hsü 郭若虛, T'u-hua chien-wen chih 圖畫見聞誌. 6 chüan. (Ferguson, 14, 1). ISTP, vol. 10, no. 66.

Kuo Jo-hsü was a minor court official at the Northern Sung capital of K'ai-feng. He was active in the middle decades of the 11th century but his exact dates are not known. In his preface to T'u-hua chien-wen chih, he relates how his grandfather and his father were enthusiastic collectors of painting and calligraphy, and although the collection was dispersed after the father's death, Kuo Jo-hsü tried and succeeded in some measure to reassemble the lost items. T'u-hua chien-wen chih is one of the standard early histories of painting, and on internal evidence may be dated to the late 1070's.

Chüan 1 is devoted to discussions of various general aspects of painting. In chüan 2-4, Kuo Jo-hsü lists and discusses 291 artists from the late T'ang to his own time. Thus, T'u-hua chien-wen chih can be used as a sequel to Chang Yen-yüan's Li-tai ming-hua chi (q.v.) as it covers the very vital 200 years between that text and Teng Ch'un's Hua chi (q.v.). Chüan 5 and 6 consist of 27 and 32 accounts of artists or well-known themes, the earliest going as far back as the 7th century and the latest touch upon events which took place in the 1070's.

The 291 artists discussed in chüan 2-4 are arranged chronologically: late T'ang, 27; Five Dynasties, 91; and Sung, 173. The last group is further divided into painters who were emperors, princes and high officials; figure and portrait painters; landscape painters; painters of birds and flowers; and miscellaneous. Each entry gives a short biography and a brief discussion of the artist's style, and notes, by title, a few of his works.

For a thorough study and translation into English of T'u-hua chien-wen chih, see Alexander Coburn Soper, Kuo Jo-hsü's Experiences in Painting (Washington, D.C., 1951).

3. Liu Tao-ch'un 劉道醇, Sheng-ch'ao ming-hua p'ing 聖朝名畫評, sometimes referred to as Sung-ch'ao ming-hua p'ing 宋朝名畫評, or Pen-ch'ao ming-hua p'ing 本朝名畫評. 3 chüan. (Ferguson, 13, 3). ISSCHC facsimile reprint of the 1908 edition (1972).

Liu Tao-ch'un's exact dates are not known. He lived in the 11th century and was probably a fairly close contemporary of Kuo Jo-hsü (q.v.). His other compilation, Wu-tai ming-hua pu-i (q.v.), has a preface dated 1060.

Sheng-ch'ao ming-hua p'ing discusses 110 painters of the early Northern Sung dynasty. They are arranged into groups according to their specialities: figure painting; landscape; animals; birds and flowers; gods and demons; and architectural painting. Within each group, the painters are graded into the "inspired", the "excellent", or the "competent" class. For each artist, there is a biography followed by a critical appraisal of his work.

4. Mi Fei 米芾, Hua shih 畫史. 1 chüan. (Ferguson, 12, 4). MSTS, vol. 10, II/9; ISTP, vol. 10, no. 68.

Mi Fei, the famous painter, calligrapher and critic, lived from 1051 to 1107. In his undated preface to Hua shih, he describes himself as an old man, and the year 1100 A.D. may be proposed as a very approximate date for its compilation.

Despite its concise title, Hua shih is not a history of painting. The work does begin with observations on painters and paintings, arranged according to dynasty, beginning with the Chin 晉. But the system soon breaks down. In the rest of the text, critical comments on paintings, both in his own collection and in other people's collections, are interspersed with comments on such related topics as silk, mounting, storage, as well as with occasional forays into such irrelevant topics as old costumes, meteorology and phonetics. However, the reader who is prepared to put up with the poor organization of the book is amply rewarded. Mi Fei's astuteness and independence as critic and his concern for the authenticity of paintings make his statements on the painters very important.

For a complete translation of Hua shih into French, see Nicole Vandier-Nicolas, Le Houa-che de Mi Fou (Paris, 1964).

5. Su Sung 蘇頌, Wei-kung t'i-pa 魏公題跋. 1 chüan. (Ferguson, 18, 1). ISTP, vol. 22, no. 174.

Su Sung (1020-1101) was an official and scholar. Wei-kung t'i-pa, culled from his collected works by the Ming bibliophile and editor Mao Chin 毛晉 (1599-1659), consists of colophons by Su on four paintings and eleven pieces of calligraphy.

6. Li Chih-i 李之儀, Ku-ch'i t'i-pa 姑溪題跋.
   2 chüan. (Ferguson, 8, 3). TSCC, no. 1593.
   [Harvard-Yenching].

   Li Chih-i was a Northern Sung scholar roughly contemporary with Su Shih 蘇軾 (1036-1101). Ku-ch'i t'i-pa consists of his colophons on one painting and 86 pieces of calligraphy.

7. Tung Yu 董逌, Kuang-ch'uan hua pa 廣川畫跋.
   6 chüan. (Ferguson, 15, 2). WSSHY, chüan 3 and 4.
   [Freer].

   Tung Yu was a late Northern Sung scholar active in the late 11th and early 12th century. Kuang-ch'uan hua-pa consists of colophons written by him on 136 paintings.

   Many of the titles are of important paintings. However, Tung Yu was a scholar rather than a connoisseur, and the colophons were merely literary exercises. He took the subject matter as a point of departure for essays, and said little of value or interest about the artists and the paintings.

   According to Hirth (Scraps from a Collector's Note Book, Leiden, 1905, pp. 113-14, the WSSHY text of Kuang-ch'uan hua pa is incomplete.

8. Chüeh-fan Te-hung 覺範德洪, <u>Shih-men t'i-pa</u> 石門題跋. 2 <u>chüan</u>. (Ferguson, 5, 6). ISTP, vol. 22, no. 180.

<u>Shih-men t'i-pa</u> records the colophons written by the monk Chüeh-fan Te-hung (1071-1128) on thirteen paintings and 100 pieces of calligraphy. The colophons embody Chan thoughts and sentiments, but virtually no information on the paintings. The work was edited by the 17th century bibliophile Mao Chin 毛晉.

9. <u>Hsüan-ho hua p'u</u> 宣和畫譜. Preface dated 1120. 20 <u>chüan</u>. (Ferguson, 9, 6). ISTP, vol. 9, no. 65.

This is the catalogue of the paintings in the imperial collection of the Northern Sung emperor Hui-tsung 徽宗 (reigned 1101-26). The preface is dated the <u>keng-tzu</u> year of the Hsüan-ho era, corresponding to 1120. Various compilers have been postulated, including Mi Fei and even Hui-tsung himself, but for none is the evidence conclusive.

A total of 6,396 paintings attributed to 231 artists, ranging from the Three Kingdoms period to Sung, are recorded. The material is divided into ten categories: (a) Buddhist and Taoist subjects (<u>chüan</u> 1-4); (b) human figures (<u>chüan</u> 5-7); (c) architecture (<u>chüan</u> 8); (d) foreigners (<u>chüan</u> 8); (e) dragons and fish (<u>chüan</u> 9); (f) landscape (<u>chüan</u> 10-12); (g) animals (<u>chüan</u> 13); (h) birds and flowers (<u>chüan</u> 15-19); (i) bamboo (<u>chüan</u> 20); and (j) vegetables (<u>chüan</u> 20).

Each category begins with an introductory section, following which the artists are arranged chronologically. For each artist, there is a biography, followed by a list of his paintings in the imperial collection. These biographies became a valuable source for later books on painting. The paintings are regrettably listed by title only and there is no other information pertaining to them.

The number of chüan devoted to the different categories do give a rough indication of their popularity and relative importance in court circles in the early 12th century. But the organization of Hsüan-ho hua p'u has its drawbacks. Cognizance is not given to the fact that a number of artists produced more than one type of painting. Once an artist is classified as of a certain category, all his paintings are listed in that category regardless of subject matter. Ku K'ai-chih is in the "Buddhist and Taoist" category, and consequently his paintings on secular subjects are grouped with his Buddhist works. Similarly, Li Kung-lin, who comes under "human figures", has his Buddhist and Taoist paintings grouped with his secular figure paintings.

10. Teng Ch'un 鄧椿 , "Ming-hsin chüeh-p'in 銘心絕品 ". (Ferguson, 14, 4). PWCSHP, chüan 97.

"Ming-hsin chüeh-p'in" is chüan 8 of Hua chi 畫繼 (preface dated 1167), a work in ten chüan by Teng Ch'un in which he sets out to provide a sequel to Chang Yen-yüan's Li-tai ming-hua chi (847 A.D.) and Kuo Jo-hsü's T'u-hua chien-wen chih (1070's) (qq.v.).

Chüan 8 is a list of 146 paintings in 37 collections which Teng Ch'un had seen; they range from the T'ang to the Sung. He stated that he had seen many more paintings but selected only the best for recording. Unfortunately they are listed by title only. The list is incorporated into P'ei-wen-chai shu hua p'u (q.v.), chüan 97.

For a discussion of Teng Ch'un's Hua chi, see Robert J. Maeda, Two Twelfth Century Texts on Chinese Painting (Michigan Papers in Chinese Studies, no. 8, 1970).

11. Yang Wang-hsiu 楊王休, Sung Chung-hsing-kuan-ko ch'u-ts'ang t'u-hua chi 宋中興館閣儲藏圖畫記. 1199 A.D. 1 chüan. (Ferguson, 7, 3). MSTS, vol. 18, IV/5; ISTP, vol. 10, no. 73.

At the end of the catalogue there is a postscript dated 1210 stating that it was compiled in 1199 by Yang Wang-hsiu (1135-1200). The short preface states: "Paintings, 187 items. The Court continues the policy of [accepting paintings as tokens of] allegiance. These paintings are combined with the 911 scrolls and two albums from the old collection formerly recorded. They are here recorded, with the [artists'] names appended."

The "old collection" and the "former catalogue" do not refer to Hui-tsung's collection recorded in Hsüan-ho hua p'u (q.v.); hardly any of the titles there are duplicated by those in Sung Chung-hsing-kuan-ko ch'u ts'ang t'u-hua chi. Rather, they refer to the Southern Sung imperial collection, a list of which, entitled Pi-ko hua mu 秘閣畫目, was compiled early in that dynasty. Much of the Northern Sung imperial collection was lost during the sack of K'ai-feng by the Chin Tartars in 1126. Kao-tsung (reigned 1127-62), the first of the Southern Sung emperors, is said to have made a serious effort to recover some of the lost paintings and to secure others, thus re-establishing another imperial collection.

In his Shu hua shu-lu chieh-t'i pu chia-pien 書畫書錄解題補甲編 (in Hua-yüan pi-chi 畫苑秘笈, pp. 2b-4a), Wu Pi-chiang 吳辟疆 puts forward cogent reasons for concluding that Pi-ko hua mu was compiled in the Shao-hsing era (1131-62). The list does not appear to have survived, presumably because its contents was incorporated into the 1199 catalogue. But a breakdown of the total of the 911 scrolls and two albums from the "old catalogue" into different categories of painting is recorded in Ch'en K'uei's 陳騤 (1128-1203) Nan-Sung kuan-ko lu 南宋館閣錄, chüan 4 (Wu-lin chang-ku 武林掌故, Taipei, 1967, p. 2728). Ch'en K'uei was the compiler of Sung Chung-hsing-kuan-ko ch'u-ts'ang shu mu 宋中興館閣儲藏書目. The two companion lists of paintings and calligraphy are preserved in Nan-Sung kuan-ko hsü-lu 南宋館閣續錄, chüan 3 (Wu-lin chang-ku, pp. 2765-72).

The 1,100 items in Sung Chung-hsing-kuan-ko ch'u-ts'ang t'u-hua chi are divided into the following categories: (1) paintings by Hui-tsung; (2) paintings bearing colophons by Hui-tsung; (3) Buddhist paintings;

(4) sages; (5) demons; (6) secular figures; (7) landscape; (8) flowers; (9) animals; and (10) insects. Within each of the categories (3) to (10), paintings are grouped by artists chronologically, followed by anonymous paintings. In categories (1) and (2), there are notations recording Hui-tsung's inscriptions and colophons.

The intrinsic interest and importance of this text are self-evident.

12. Chu Hsi 朱熹, Hui-an t'i-pa 晦庵題跋. 3 chüan. (Ferguson, 11, 2). ISTP, vol. 23, no. 183.

Hui-an t'i-pa records colophons on five paintings and 208 pieces of calligraphy by Chu Hsi (1130-1200), the eminent neo-Confucianist philosopher. The work was edited by Mao Chin (q.v.).

13. Ch'en Fu-liang 陳傅良, Chih-chai t'i-pa 止齋題跋. 2 chüan. (Ferguson, 4, 4). ISTP, vol. 23, no. 184.

Ch'en Fu-liang (1141-1207) was a scholar and official, but not, judging from Chih-chai t'i-pa, a connoisseur of painting. Only nine of the 54 colophons recorded are on paintings, and the remarks are inconsequential.

14. Yeh Shih 葉適, Shui-hsin t'i-pa 水心題跋. 1 chüan. (Ferguson, 4, 5). ISTP, vol. 23, no. 185.

Yeh Shih (1150-1223) was a scholar and official. The inclusion of <u>Shui-hsin t'i-pa</u> in Ferguson's bibliography is puzzling. Only three of the 55 colophons and encomiums were on paintings. The three paintings are not identified by artists, nor do they seem to be entered in the "Anonymous" section of <u>Li-tai chu-lu hua-mu</u>. The work was edited by Mao Chin (<u>q.v.</u>).

15. Chou Mi 周密, <u>Yün-yen kuo-yen lu</u> 雲烟過眼錄. 2 <u>chüan</u>. (Ferguson, 12, 11). MSTS, vol. 6, II/2; ISTP, vol. 17, no. 152.

Chou Mi (1232-ca. 1308), scholar, poet and connoisseur, was an important figure of the period of late Southern Sung to early Yüan. <u>Yün-yen kuo-yen lu</u> is a catalogue of the paintings, calligraphy, bronzes, jades, ceramics and musical instruments in 45 collections which he had seen. The title is an allusion to an essay by Su Shih in which he compares old paintings to clouds which drift before the eyes.

Paintings and calligraphy constitute the majority of the items recorded. The entries for the paintings vary greatly in length. Some are merely titles while others record approximate dimensions and transcribe colophons and seals. This is something of an innovation. We would naturally wish for a more consistent treatment of all the paintings and for some critical comments from such an eminent connoisseur, but at that relatively early date, the cataloguing of paintings was still in its infancy.

16. T'ang Yün-mo 湯允謨, Yün-yen kuo-yen hsü-lu 雲烟過眼續錄. 1 chüan. (Ferguson, 12, 12). MSTS, vol. 6, II/2; ISTP, vol. 17, no. 153.

T'ang Yün-mo lived in the Yüan dynasty. The work is a sequel to Chou Mi's Yün-yen kuo-yen lu (q.v.), and follows it in organization. It records the paintings, bronzes, jades and other antiquities in four collections. The paintings are very few in number.

17. Yüan Chüeh 袁桷, "Lu-kuo Ta-chang-kung-chu t'u-hua chi 魯國大長公主圖畫記". (Ferguson, 15, 3). PWCSHP, chüan 97.

This is a list of the titles of 35 paintings in the collection of the Yüan dynasty princess Hsiang-ko-la-chi 祥哥拉吉 (Sengge Ragi). She was a niece and daughter-in-law of Tämur 鐵穆耳 (Ch'eng-tsung, reigned 1295-1307), the younger sister of Haisan 海山 (Wu-tsung, reigned 1308-1311), and older sister of Ayurparibhadra 愛育黎拔力八達 (Jen-tsung, reigned 1312-1320).

The list is excerpted from Ch'ing-jung-chu-shih chi 清容居士集 by Yüan Chüeh (1266-1327), and records how the Princess had gathered together some courtiers, feasted them, and asked them to write colophons on the paintings. The event took place in 1323. The list appears in P'ei-wen-chai shu hua p'u (q.v.), chüan 97.

18. Chu Ts'un-li 朱存理, Shan-hu mu-nan 珊瑚木難. 8 chüan. (Ferguson, 9, 8). ISSCHC facsimile reprint of the manuscript copy in the National Central Library (1970).

Chu Ts'un-li (1444-1513) was a scholar and connoisseur, and he was friendly with Shen Chou 沈周 and his circle. Shan-hu mu-nan is a record of the inscriptions and colophons on the paintings and calligraphy he had seen. Often he would state where he had seen the painting or calligraphy, or from where he had borrowed it to transcribe the colophons. There is no other information on the paintings.

The arrangement of the text leaves much to be desired. Paintings and calligraphy are interspersed, and there is no chronological order. The value of the text lies in the importance given to inscriptions and colophons, which constituted something of an innovation and became standard practice in many subsequent catalogues.

19. Tu Mu 都穆, Yü-i pien 寓意編. 1 chüan. (Ferguson, 12, 1). MSTS, vol. 6, II/1; ISTP, vol. 17, no. 155.

Tu Mu (1458-1525) was a noted scholar and connoisseur in Suchou, and he was friendly with Shen Chou and such members of his circle as Liu Chüeh 劉珏 and Wu K'uan 吳寬. Yü-i pien consists of notes on 60 paintings and some calligraphy which he had seen in various collections.

The material is arranged in random fashion and the entries are not standardized. Some paintings are listed by title only while others have information on colophons, seals and pedigree. The comments are interesting because of the circle in which Tu Mu moved and because some of the paintings are important.

20. Hua Hsia 華夏 , "Hua shih Chen-shang-chai fu chu 華氏真賞齋賦注". (Ferguson, 12, 8). PWCSHP, chüan 98.

Hua Hsia (born ca. 1498, chin-shih 1544) was a collector and connoisseur. "Hua shih Chen-shang-chai fu chu" is a short list of 14 paintings ranging from the T'ang to the Yüan in his collection. The list appears in P'ei-wen-chai shu hua p'u (q.v.), chüan 98.

21. Wen Chia 文嘉 , Ch'ien-shan-t'ang shu hua chi 鈐山堂書畫記. Preface dated 1569. 1 chüan. (Ferguson, 12, 10). MSTS, vol. 8, II/6; ISTP, vol. 17, no. 156.

At the end of the work is a postscript by Wen Chia (1501-83) dated 1569 stating that Ch'ien-shan-t'ang shu hua chi is a list of the paintings and calligraphy confiscated from Yen Sung 嚴嵩 (1480-1565).

Grand Secretary from 1542 to 1562, Yen Sung was a great favourite of the Chia-ching emperor and wielded immense power. Towards the end of his life, a combination of forces brought about his downfall. He came under fierce attack from his enemies, was dismissed from office, and degraded to the status of a commoner. One of the accusations brought against him was the inordinate tribute he exacted for favours, and the booty he amassed was all confiscated on his dismissal from office.

In his postscript Wen Chia states: "In the fifth month of the i-ch'ou year in the reign of Chia-ching [1565], Mr. Ho Pin-yai 何賓涯 the t'i-hsüeh 提學 asked me to go over the confiscated paintings and calligraphy from Yen's old residence at Fen-i 分宜 and his new residences at Yüan-chou 袁州 and the provincial capital. It took three months for me to go through these and even then I could no more than glance at them cursorily. Recently while sorting my papers, I came across the list, and so I made a catalogue with some notations....Wen Chia."

Because of his wealth and power, Yen Sung was indeed able to amass a large and very important collection of painting and calligraphy. The paintings, occupying the second half of the catalogue, are arranged chronologically and they range from Chin 晉 to Ming. Many of the paintings are listed by title only, but others have brief comments comparing them to other versions known to the compiler. For these reasons, the catalogue is of considerable interest despite the fact that it could be far more informative.

22. "Yen shih shu hua chi 嚴氏書畫記". (Ferguson, 20, 1). PWCSHP, chüan 98.

This is a list of the paintings and calligraphy in the collection of Yen Sung (q.v.). The paintings are listed by artist and title only. Culled from Wen Chia's Ch'ien-shan-t'ang shu hua chi (q.v.), the list first appeared in Shan-hu-wang hua lu (q.v.), chüan 23, and was later incorporated into Shih-ku-t'ang shu hua hui-k'ao (q.v.), chüan 2, and P'ei-wen-chai shu hua p'u (q.v.), chüan 98.

23. Chou Shih-lin 周石林, T'ien-shui ping-shan lu 天水冰山錄. 1 chüan. (Ferguson, 4, 3). CPTCTS, nos. 108-112. [Freer].

Although this work bears the name of Chou Shih-lin, an early Ch'ing man, as its compiler, it is based on a manuscript copy of Ming date. The compilation consists of a list of all of Yen Sung's (q.v.) properties, as distinct from Wen-chia's Ch'ien-shan-t'ang shu hua lu (q.v.) which lists Yen Sung's paintings and calligraphy only.

24. Ho Liang-chün 何良俊, "Shu hua ming-hsin lu 書畫銘心錄". Postscript dated 1567. (Ferguson, 10, 4). PWCSHP, chüan 98.

This short text is attributed to the Ming scholar Ho Liang-chün who was active in the Chia-ching period. His exact dates are not known, but his younger brother,

Ho Liang-fu 何良傅, lived from 1509 to 1562. "Shu hua ming-hsin lu" does not exist as an independent work, but appears in P'ei-wen-chai shu hua p'u (q.v.), chüan 98, as well as in T'ieh-wang shan-hu (q.v., No. 63), which is a questionable text. These versions differ considerably. In the latter version, there is a preface dated 1556 and a postscript dated 1567.

The text records several dozen paintings of Yüan and early Ming date seen in four collections. Many of the entries contain descriptions of the paintings and critical comments. Occasionally approximate dimensions are given and important colophons noted but not transcribed.

25. Wang Shih-chen 王世貞, Yen-chou-shan-jen kao 弇州山人稿; 176 chüan. Yen-chou-shan-jen hsü-kao 弇州山人續稿; 207 chüan. (Ferguson, 9, 7). 1577 edition and Wan-li edition respectively. [Library of Congress].

Yen-chou-shan-jen kao and hsü-kao are a collection of the writings of Wang Shih-chen (1526-90), the eminent scholar, bibliophile and connoisseur.

Only chüan 137 and 138 in kao and chüan 168-70 in hsü-kao need concern us. In these five chüan are recorded colophons written by Wang Shih-chen on 183 paintings, ranging from T'ang to Ming. They contain interesting comments of a critical and scholarly nature; there is no other information on the paintings. Many of the paintings were important ones and some of them are still extant.

26. Wang Shih-chen 王世貞, "Wang Shih-chen Erh-ya-lou so-ts'ang ming-hua 王世貞爾雅樓所藏名畫". (Ferguson, 4, 6). PWCSHP, chüan 98.

This is a list of the paintings in the collection of Wang Shih-chen (1526-1590), culled from his Yen-chou-shan-jen kao (q.v.). The list has little information apart from the titles of the paintings.

The list first appeared in this form in Shan-hu-wang hua lu (q.v.), chüan 23. It was later incorporated into Shih-ku-t'ang shu hua hui-k'ao (q.v.), chüan 2, and into P'ei-wen-chai shu hua p'u (q.v.), chüan 98.

27. Wang Shih-mou 王世懋, "Wang Shih-mou Tan-pu hua p'in 王世懋澹圃畫品". (Ferguson, 4, 7). PWCSHP, chüan 98.

This is a list of the paintings in the collection of Wang Shih-chen's younger brother, Wang Shih-mou (1536-1588), culled from his Wang Feng-ch'ang chi 王奉常集. There is little information apart from titles of paintings.

The list first appeared in this form in Shan-hu-wang hua lu (q.v.), chüan 23. It was later incorporated into Shih-ku-t'ang shu hua hui-k'ao (q.v.), chüan 2, and into P'ei-wen-chai shu hua p'u (q.v.), chüan 98.

28. Chan Ching-feng 詹景鳳, Tung-t'u hsüan-lan pien 東圖玄覽編. Preface dated 1591. 4 chüan. (Ferguson, 8, 5). MSTS, vol. 21, V/1; ISSCHC facsimile reprint of the manuscript copy in the National Central Library (1970).

Chan Ching-feng (chü-jen 1567) was a painter, calligrapher and connoisseur active in the latter part of the 16th century. Tung-t'u hsüan-lan pien, originally in 30 chüan, was never printed in its entirety. Only four of the 30 chüan are concerned with painting and calligraphy, the remaining chüan consist of poems, essays and miscellaneous notes.

The four chüan have little organization. They record about 400 paintings and roughly the same number of calligraphy which Chan Ching-feng had seen in various collections. Prominent among these are those of Han Shih-neng, Wang Shih-chen and his brother Wang Shih-mou (qq.v.), who must have been his close contemporaries. The entries vary a great deal in length, from one or two lines to very detailed records, containing all the information which one is likely to want from a catalogue, as well as critical comments and anecdotes on how certain paintings changed hands.

This is an interesting text. Many of the paintings are important and some of them are still extant. It is not easy to use because there is no table of contents, but a leisurely perusal of the contents should be rewarding.

Ferguson did not adequately index the paintings recorded in this text. He used the incomplete list as it appears in P'ei-wen-chai shu hua p'u (q.v.), chüan 99. Reference should therefore be made to either of the two editions here cited. The MSTS edition states that the manuscript copy on which it is based has a preface dated 1591. The same edition includes a supplement consisting of 38 colophons by Chan on paintings, culled from the other 26 chüan of Tung-t'u hsüan-lan pien. No such supplement is in the 1970 reprint.

29. Sun Kung 孫鑛, Shu hua pa pa 書畫跋跋.
3 chüan, supplement 3 chüan. (Ferguson, 10, 3).
ISSCHC facsimile reprint of the 1919 edition (1970).

Sun Kung (1542-1613) was a scholar and official. Shu hua pa pa is a commentary on some of the colophons by Wang Shih-chen (1526-1590) on paintings and calligraphy collected under the title of Yen-chou-shan-jen t'i-pa 弇州山人題跋 and incorporated into Wang Shih-chen's miscellaneous writings in Yen-chou-shan-jen kao (q.v.).

Shu hua pa pa existed in manuscript form until 1739 when it was printed for the first time under the auspices of two of Sun Kung's sixth generation descendants.

Sixty-five and 18 colophons on paintings are dealt with respectively in chüan 3 and supplement chüan 3; the rest of the text is devoted to calligraphy. In each entry, Wang Shih-chen's colophon is transcribed in small characters and Sun Kung's comments are in large characters. The text is of minimal interest. Far from subjecting Wang Shih-chen's pronouncements to a critical evaluation, which would have served a certain purpose since Wang Shih-chen was an important critic, the comments are inconsequential.

30. Chu Ts'un-li 朱存理 [sic., Chao Ch'i-mei 趙琦美], T'ieh-wang shan-hu 鐵網珊瑚. Postscript dated 1600. 16 chüan. (Ferguson, 20, 3). ISSCHC facsimile reprint of manuscript copy in the National Central Library (1970).

This text was attributed to Chu Ts'un-li (1444-1513) (q.v.) and still bears his name on the cover of the 1970 reprint. However, it is now generally agreed that the text was assembled by Chao Ch'i-mei (1563-1624), the well-known bibliophile and book collector.

Some editions of the text have a postscript dated 1600 by Chao Ch'i-mei stating that he had combined two anonymous texts borrowed from his friends Ch'in Ssu-lin 秦四麟 and Chiao Hung 焦竑 (1541-1620), re-arranged the entries, and added some of his own. These editorial actions by Chao are deplorable as they render it impossible to sort out the contributions from the three different sources and arrive at a more correct dating of them. One or both of the anonymous texts could well have been from the early part of Ming, although it is impossible to say if they had any association with Chu Ts'un-li.

Chüan 1-10 are on calligraphy, and chüan 11-16 on painting. So far as can be ascertained from the text, there is an unevenness in the quality of the paintings, as is understandable in a text of diverse origins. The majority of the paintings are Sung and Yüan. Some of them are important paintings, and a number of them can be identified with extant paintings. The entries do not contain catalogue information such as dimensions, materials and seals, nor do they have descriptions of the paintings. As in Shan-hu mu-nan (q.v.), inscriptions and colophons are fully transcribed, and perhaps that is the reason why the text was attributed to Chu Ts'un-li.

31. Chao Ch'i-mei 趙琦美, Mai-wang-kuan shu mu 脈望館書目. 1 chüan. (Ferguson, 9, 11). HFLPC, vi. [Harvard-Yenching].

Chao Ch'i-mei (1563-1624) was an avid book collector. Mai-wang-kuan shu mu is an inventory of his extensive library plus a list of about 35 paintings and various antiquities in his collection. The paintings bear attributions to T'ang through Ming, and are listed by title only.

32. Mao Wei 茅維, "Nan-yang ming-hua piao 南陽名畫表". (Ferguson, 9, 4). PWCSHP, chüan 100.

This list of 99 paintings by 47 artists in the collection of Han Shih-neng 韓世能 (1528-1598) appears in P'ei-wen-chai shu hua p'u (q.v.), chüan 100. The compiler is given as Mao Wei, a scholar and poet who was active in the early 17th century. The list is virtually the same as Chang Ch'ou's Nan-yang ming-hua piao (q.v.). The wording of the short preface suggests that it was lifted from Chang Ch'ou's longer preface and raises the possibility of the list itself being based on Chang Ch'ou's list rather than being compiled independently.

33. Chang Ch'ou 張丑, <u>Nan-yang ming-hua piao</u> 南陽名畫表. (Ferguson, 9, 3). CSSHSP. [Freer].

This is a list of 95 paintings by 47 artists in the collection of Han Shih-neng 韓世能 (1528-1598), compiled sometime after his death. Han Shih-neng was a high official whose last position before retirement was that of Vice Minister in the Board of Rites, and he was a most prominent collector, much admired by Chang Ch'ou.

The list is tabulated into columns: the vertical ones for the dynasties, from the period of the Three Kingdoms to the Yüan, and the horizontal ones for (a) Buddhist, Taoist and secular figure paintings, (b) landscape and architectural paintings, (c) flowers and birds, and (d) insects and fish. The paintings are listed by title, and many of them have a terse statement noting important colophons.

34. Chang Ch'ou 張丑, <u>Ch'ing-ho shu hua piao</u> 清河書畫表, sometimes referred to as <u>Ch'ing-ho pi-ch'ieh shu hua piao</u> 清河秘篋書畫表. 1 <u>chüan</u>. (Ferguson, 11, 3). CSSHSP. [Freer].

This is a list compiled by Chang Ch'ou (1577-1643) of 115 paintings and 49 pieces of calligraphy in the collections of eight members of six generations of his family. In his preface, Chang Ch'ou states that for generations his family had been closely associated with the foremost painters of their day. Great-grandfather Tzu-ho 子和 and his older brother Wei-ch'ing 維慶 are said to have been friendly with Shen Chou. Grandfather Yüeh-chih 約之 and his younger brother Ch'eng-chih 誠之 were on intimate terms with Wen Chengming, and this bond was sealed when the families were united by marriage in the next generation.

The material is tabulated into seven horizontal columns and eight vertical columns. Each of the horizontal columns designates a generation: (1) great-great-grandfather Yüan-su 元素; (2) great-grandfather Tzu-ho and his older brother Wei-ch'ing; (3) grandfather Yüeh-chih and his younger brother Ch'eng-chih; (4) father Mou-shih 茂實; (5) cousin I-sheng 以繩; (6) Chang Ch'ou himself; (7) nephew Tan-chia 誕嘉. The vertical columns are drawn up according to the dynasties, from Chin 晉 to Ming.

The value of this text is limited as the items are listed by title only.

35. Chang Ch'ou 張丑, Shu hua chien wen piao 書畫見聞表, sometimes referred to as Fa-shu ming-hua chien wen piao 法書名畫見聞表. 1 chüan. (Ferguson, 10, 2). CSSHSP. [Freer].

This is a list of 265 paintings and 188 pieces of calligraphy which Chang Ch'ou (1577-1643) had seen or heard about, compiled probably before Ch'ing-ho shu hua fang (q.v.). The paintings range from the Six Dynasties to Ming, and are arranged chronologically with the calligraphy, but divided into two categories, those which Chang Ch'ou had seen and those which he only knew about. The works are listed by title only and there is no other information.

36. Chang Ch'ou 張丑, Ch'ing-ho shu hua fang 清河書畫舫. Preface 1616. 12 chüan. (Ferguson, 11, 4). 1875 edition. [Freer].

Coming as he did from a family of collectors who were on friendly terms with artists and collectors of their time, Chang Ch'ou (1577-1643) (q.v.) had the opportunity of seeing a large number of important paintings and calligraphy. Ch'ing-ho shu hua fang is a catalogue of a large number of paintings and calligraphy ranging from the Three Kingdoms period to Ming.

Unfortunately, the text is marred by many flaws. While it is understandable that Chang Ch'ou should include paintings he had not seen in an unpretentious list such as Shu hua chien wen piao (q.v.), their inclusion in a text of much more serious intent is of very dubious value. The same fuzziness of purpose is probably responsible for inconsistencies in the organization, rendering the text difficult to use.

The broad scheme of the text is as follows. The material is arranged by period and within each period by individual painter or calligrapher. For each artist, Chang Ch'ou begins with an introductory section bringing together general information on him culled from his wide reading. Following this is a catalogue of the works he had seen or heard about. Chang Ch'ou would record when and in whose collection he saw a painting. There is no catalogue information such as dimensions, materials and description of the painting. Inscriptions and colophons are fully transcribed but seals are only infrequently recorded. In the cases where Chang Ch'ou had not seen the paintings, the transcriptions were drawn from texts. Almost always, an entry would be followed by quotations from earlier texts on the painting. Often at the end of a chüan, there would be supplements on various artists dealt with in the same chüan, with information on additional paintings and lengthy quotations from Hsüan-ho hua p'u (q.v.), including all the titles by the artists listed there.

The inclusion of such texts as Mi Fei's Pao-chang tai-fang lu 寶章待訪錄 and Wen Chia's Yen shih shu hua chi (q.v.) in the sections devoted to these artists is yet another proof that Chang Ch'ou's Ch'ing-ho shu hua fang is extremely ill-defined in purpose.

The defects apart, this text is interesting for its quotations on paintings from some early, relatively unknown, texts; for its full transcriptions of colophons on those paintings Chang Ch'ou had actually seen; and for the occasional comments by Chang Ch'ou on paintings and personalities.

37. Chang Ch'ou 張丑 , Chen-chi jih lu 真蹟日錄.
    3 chüan. (Ferguson, 10, 7). 1918 edition.
    [Library of Congress].

According to Chang Ch'ou's preface, so many paintings and calligraphy were shown to him after he finished Ch'ing-ho shu hua fang (q.v.) that he kept notes on some of them, and the result was Chen-chi jih lu. As the title indicates, the text is in diary form recording the items in the order in which Chang saw them. Not every entry is dated, but the few dates which can be found are in correspondence with the 1620's, and the text can be assigned to that decade.

About 160 paintings and 130 pieces of calligraphy ranging from the Six Dynasties to the Ming are recorded in Chen-chi jih lu. The entries follow no fixed form and vary in length according to whether Chang Ch'ou found them interesting. Many entries are lengthy and contain transcriptions of colophons as well as record seals; they often end with a critical comment by Chang Ch'ou. The owners of many of the items are identified. Perusal of this text can be rewarding.

38. Li Jih-hua 李日華, Liu-yen-chai pi-chi 六硯齋筆記, 4 chüan; Liu-yen-chai erh-pi 六硯齋二筆, 4 chüan; Liu-yen-chai san-pi 六硯齋三筆, 4 chüan. (Ferguson, 4, 2). KHCPWK. [Asia Library, University of Michigan].

Li Jih-hua (1565-1635) was a scholar and connoisseur. Liu-yen-chai pi-chi and its two sequels are a miscellany in the form of an informal diary recording events and thoughts on such diverse topics as Taoism, medicine, poetry and the arts as they occurred to him between the years 1624 and 1635.

Much of the text is concerned with paintings and calligraphy which he saw, and these entries are often quite detailed, recording artist, title, subject matter and colophons. The book is also full of titbits of information of peripheral interest, such as the identification of persons and studios. It is the kind of text that would reward any casual browsing.

39. Tung Ch'i-ch'ang 董其昌, <u>Jung-t'ai pieh-chi 容臺別集</u>. 6 <u>chüan</u>. (Ferguson, 10, 1). MTISCWCHK facsimile reprint of the original edition in the National Central Library, vol. 14. [Freer].

<u>Jung-t'ai pieh-chi</u> is a sequel to <u>Jung-t'ai chi</u> 容臺集, a collection of the miscellaneous writings of Tung Ch'i-ch'ang (1555-1636). Both were compiled by his grandson Tung T'ing 董庭. Although the preface to <u>Jung-t'ai pieh-chi</u> has no date, its compilation is probably not much later than that of <u>Jung-t'ai chi</u> which has a preface by Ch'en Chi-ju (<u>q.v.</u>) dated 1630.

Scattered in <u>chüan</u> 1, 2 and 6 are a number of colophons on paintings by Tung Ch'i-ch'ang, some in his own collection and others seen by him. Since Tung Ch'i-ch'ang was such an eminent painter and critic, the statements he made on earlier painters are of extreme importance. There is no catalogue information of the usual sort, only critical comments.

Instead of indexing all the titles of paintings discussed in pieh-chi, Ferguson lists only the few titles quoted in P'ei-wen-chai shu hua p'u (q.v.), chüan 100 and one or two other places in that anthology.

40. Tung Ch'i-ch'ang 董其昌, Hua-chan-shih sui-pi 畫禪室隨筆. 1 chüan. (Ferguson, 12, 5). 1720 edition in ISTP, vol. 28, no. 252.

Hua-chan-shih sui-pi is a selection of the writings of Tung Ch'i-ch'ang (1555-1636), compiled by Yang Wu-pu 楊無補 (died 1657). Very little material in this selection duplicates that in Jung-t'ai chi and pieh-chi (qq.v.), and it is probable that the selection was made to supplement them.

There are 16 sections in Hua-chan-shih sui-pi. Ferguson uses only the abbreviated version of section 6, entitled "Hua yüan 畫源", as given in P'ei-wen-chai shu hua-p'u (q.v.), chüan 100, but reference should be made to the fuller original text. In it, Tung Ch'i-ch'ang discusses about 50 paintings, some in his collection and others he had seen. They are all important monuments.

Two other sections in Hua-chan-shih sui-pi are relevant to our purpose; they were not indexed by Ferguson. These are: section 7, entitled "T'i tzu hua 題自畫", which consists of 43 inscriptions on Tung Ch'i-ch'ang's own paintings; and section 8, entitled "P'ing chiu hua 評舊畫", which consists of 17 colophons by Tung on earlier paintings.

41. Chang T'ai-chieh 張泰階, Pao hui lu 寶繪錄, sometimes referred to as Ssu-ch'ao pao hui lu 四朝寶繪錄. Preface dated 1633. 20 chüan. (Ferguson, 19, 2). ISSCHC facsimile reprint of the CPTCTS edition (1972).

Chang T'ai-chieh obtained his chin-shih degree in 1619. Apart from some general statements on paintings and certain painters in chüan 1, Pao hui lu is a catalogue of several hundred paintings attributed to the foremost painters of the Six Dynasties, the T'ang, the Sung and the Yüan dynasties. Hence the "ssu-ch'ao" of the title. The probability of so many paintings by the best artists from the 5th to the 14th century being genuine is very slight indeed, and one cannot help but be very sceptical of their authenticity. In Ch'ing-hsia-kuan lun hua chüeh-chü (q.v.), Wu Hsiu baldly states that Chang T'ai-chieh was an unscrupulous dealer and that all the paintings recorded in Pao hui lu were recent forgeries.

The entries record only inscriptions and colophons. Regardless of whether the paintings were genuine or not, the lack of such information as dimensions, materials, seals, and so on, makes the text hopelessly inadequate as a catalogue.

42. Yü Feng-ch'ing 郁逢慶, Yü shih shu hua t'i-pa chi 郁氏書畫題跋記. Postscript dated 1633. 12 chüan. (Ferguson, 9, 13). ISSCHC facsimile reprint of manuscript copy in the National Central Library (1970).

Yü Feng-ch'ing was a connoisseur active in the late Ming dynasty. In his postscript dated 1633, he relates how the book grew out of transcriptions he made over the years of inscriptions and colophons on paintings and calligraphy which belonged to his collector friends. Paintings and calligraphy are not put into separate categories, nor are they arranged in chronological order. They are presumably in the order in which Yü saw them.

The text is of limited value because it contains no more information on the paintings than selected inscriptions and colophons. Consequently it is difficult to be certain of the relationship between the paintings in the text and extant paintings with the same or similar titles.

In certain editions of this text, there is a supplement of twelve more chüan.

43. Ch'en Chi-ju 陳繼儒, Ni ku lu 妮古錄.
    4 chüan. (Ferguson, 8, 2). MSTS, vol. 5, I/10; ISTP, vol. 29, no. 253.

Ch'en Chi-ju (1558-1639) was a late Ming painter, and a contemporary and close friend of Tung Ch'i-ch'ang (q.v.). Ni ku lu is in the form of notes on paintings, calligraphy and other antiquities in his own and other people's collections. The notes, written in and about 1635, are in the order in which the objects were seen. Hence, the material is not well organized, and sometimes the same items are discussed in two different entries.

There is no complete catalogue information on the paintings, and the comments are in the nature of a painter's opinions.

44. Wang K'o-yü 汪砢玉, Shan-hu-wang hua lu 珊瑚網畫錄. Preface dated 1643. 24 chüan, supplement 1 chüan. (Ferguson, 9, 9). 1916 edition. [Freer]. Chüan 23 appears under the title of Hua chü 畫據 in MSTS, vol. 6, II/1 and ISTP, vol. 13, no. 106; chüan 24 appears under the title of Hua chi 畫繼 in MSTS, vol. 6, II/1 and ISTP, vol. 13, no. 105; the supplement appears under the title of Hua fa 畫法 in MSTS, vol. 6, II/1 and ISTP, vol. 13, no. 107.

Wang K'o-yü (born 1587) came from a family with a long tradition of collecting. His father Wang Ai-ching 汪愛荊 was a contemporary and close friend of the eminent collector Hsiang Yüan-pien 項元汴 (1525-90). Consequently, apart from inheriting his father's collection, Wang K'o-yü no doubt had the opportunity of seeing at least part of Hsiang's extraordinary collection.

Chüan 1-22 of Shan-hu-wang hua lu are devoted to recording the inscriptions and colophons on a large number of paintings, some in Wang's own collection, some seen by him, and others which he knew of from reading. Unfortunately, Wang does not give dimensions, nor information on materials and seals. The paintings range in date from the Six Dynasties to the Ming, and they are arranged chronologically, album leaves being relegated to chüan 19-22.

Chüan 23 consists of a list of paintings in a number of famous collections in the Sung, Yüan and Ming dynasties, compiled from various earlier texts. It is the source of many subsequent lists of this nature, such as that in Shih-ku-t'ang shu hua hui-k'ao, in Chu-chia ts'ang-hua pu and in P'ei-wen-chai shu hua p'u (qq.v.). Chüan 24 consists of quotations from various writers on the theory of painting and a survey of the history of painting. The last chüan, the supplement, is a manual on painting, culled from earlier writings.

45. Chu Chih-ch'ih 朱之赤, Chu Wo-an ts'ang shu hua mu 朱臥菴藏書畫目. 1 chüan. (Ferguson, 6, 3). MSTS, vol. 8, II/6; ISTP, vol. 17, no. 157.

The dates of Chu Chih-ch'ih's birth and death are not known. He is generally considered a Ming man, but there is evidence for his having lived into the Ch'ing dynasty. One entry in Chu Wo-an ts'ang shu hua mu refers to Wang To 王鐸 (1592-1652) by his posthumous title, so that we can say that this text is no earlier than 1652.

The text is little more than a list of the titles of the paintings and calligraphy in Chu Chih-ch'ih's collection. The only additional information is the mention of notable colophons.

In his Shu hua shu-lu chieh-t'i (q.v., chüan 6:16a), Yü Shao-sung questions the authenticity of this text on the basis of an entry for "a landscape by Ku T'ing-lin

顧亭林 after Huang Kung-wang, with a colophon by Ch'en Chi-ju". Yü Shao-sung maintains that Ku T'ing-lin, whom he mistook for Ku Yen-wu 顧炎武, a calligrapher who lived from 1613 to 1682, was much too junior to Ch'en Chi-ju (1558-1639) in years to have a colophon by the eminent painter on his painting if he had indeed been able to produce a painting. However, Ku T'ing-lin was probably Ku Cheng-i 顧正誼, who was indeed a landscape painter and a contemporary of Ch'en Chi-ju. Both Ku Cheng-i and Ku Yen-wu had T'ing-lin as their hao.

46. Sun Ch'eng-tse 孫承澤, Keng-tzu hsiao-hsia chi 庚子銷夏記. 1660. 8 chüan. (Ferguson, 8, 4). ISSCHC facsimile reprint of the 1761 edition (1970).

Sun Ch'eng-tse (1592-1676) was a scholar and official who served under both the Ming and Ch'ing governments. Keng-tzu hsiao-hsia chi was written in his retirement in the summer of the keng-tzu year, corresponding to 1660.

Chüan 1-3 record Sun's collection of paintings and calligraphy ranging from the Six Dynasties to the Ming. Chüan 4-7 deal with pei, stone engravings of calligraphy, and t'ieh, reproductions of famous calligraphy. Chüan 8 records paintings and calligraphy in other people's collections which Sun had seen.

The text is weak on catalogue information and strong on critical comments and research. Sun Ch'eng-tse does not concern himself with such matters as measurements, materials, seals and colophons. He combines connoisseurship with research, and the entries consist of critical evaluation of the items and information on the artists' life and other works.

47. Pien Yung-yü 卞永譽, Shih-ku-t'ang shu hua hui-k'ao 式古堂書畫彙考. 1682. 60 chüan. (Ferguson, 6, 2). Facsimile reprint of the original K'ang-hsi edition (1921). [Freer]. Facsimile reprint of the 1921 reprint (Taipei, 1958).

Pien Yung-yü (1645-1712) was a senior official and from his youth was interested in painting and calligraphy. He knew many of the prominent collectors of his time and had the opportunity of studying many original masterpieces and making notes on what he saw.

While serving as Intendant of Couriers in Shantung in the years 1680-82, Pien Yung-yü compiled Shih-ku-t'ang shu hua hui-k'ao, an ambitious work which set out to be a more comprehensive text of painting and calligraphy than had hitherto been attempted. For this he consulted more than 130 books, collating the information on each item he listed. The work is in 60 chüan, 30 of which are devoted to calligraphy and 30 to painting. For the latter, the books consulted number ninety.

Chüan 1 is an anthology of quotations on the theory of painting from various old texts on the subject. Chüan 2 records 82 famous collections, imperial and private, from the T'ang to Ming. Much of this information is taken verbatim from Shan-hu-wang hua lu (q.v.), chüan 23. The paintings in the 82 collections are listed by title only. Chüan 3-7 record famous albums, and chüan 8-30 famous handscrolls and hanging scrolls, arranged under their artists, who are placed in a chronological sequence. For those items which Pien had actually seen, inscriptions and colophons are conscientiously transcribed and seals are fully recorded. Such catalogue information as dimensions, materials, subject matter and description of painting is terse and could be more fully and consistently given. These parts of the text are useful.

For those paintings which Pien had not seen, he would have a "wai-lu 外錄 " section in which he quotes from various sources where the paintings are recorded or discussed. Consequently, Shih-ku-t'ang is often used as an index to the books which Pien lists in his bibliography. As such, the text should be used with caution, as these quotations are not always judiciously chosen nor are they exhaustive in relaying the information in the books consulted.

A single example will suffice to demonstrate these shortcomings. In chüan 8, Ku K'ai-chih section, pp. 4b-5b (1958 reprint, vol. 3, p. 351), the painting entitled Lo-shen t'u (Nymph of the Lo River) has in its entry two quotations. The second is a lengthy quotation from Kuo Ju-hsü's T'u-hua chien-wen chih (q.v.) which does not mention the Lo-shen t'u. The quotation is therefore entirely irrelevant, and its presence may even mislead a casual reader into thinking that the Lo-shen t'u is recorded in T'u-hua chien-wen chih as being in

Ku K'ai-chih's oeuvre. In actual fact, the artist whose name is more firmly associated with the Lo-shen t'u in early texts is Ssu-ma Chao 司馬昭 (299-325) who reigned as Chin Ming-ti 晉明帝 from 323 to 325. The two early texts which furnish this piece of evidence are P'ei Hsiao-yüan's Chen-kuan kung ssu hua shih and Chang Yen-yüan's Li-tai ming-hua chi (qq.v.). While both these texts are in Pien Yung-yü's extensive bibliography, only the former is quoted by him in the section on Chin Ming-ti (chüan 8; 1958 reprint, vol. 3, p. 348). The omission of latter reference, the absence of an entry for the Lo-shen t'u in its own right in the section on Chin Ming-ti, plus the misleading long quotation from T'u-hua chien-wen chih in the Ku K'ai-chih section — these are tantamount to a gross distortion of the evidence. One reason for these errors of omission and commission may be that by Pien Yung-yü's time, the Lo-shen t'u was so firmly attributed to Ku K'ai-chih that any evidence to the contrary would be too disturbing for comfort. And by so injudiciously using the textual evidence at his disposal, Pien further compounded the impression of a firm association of Ku K'ai-chih with the painting.

The conclusion must be that Shih-ku-t'ang shu hua hui-k'ao fails to fulfil its potential as Pien Yung-yü lacked the qualities of accuracy, thoroughness and truthfulness necessary for a compilation of this kind. The parts dealing with paintings which Pien had not seen can be used as a lead to some of the older texts, but the reader is urged to verify the sources rather than stop at Shih-ku-t'ang.

48. Yün Shou-p'ing 惲壽平, Nan-t'ien hua pa 南田畫跋. 4 chüan. (Ferguson, 9, 1). MSTS, vol. 18, LV/6; ISTP, vol. 23, no. 198.

Yün Shou-p'ing (1633-1690) was one of the painters of the so-called orthodox school of the early Ch'ing dynasty. Nan-t'ien hua pa is a collection of the random thoughts of Yün Shou-p'ing on the painters and paintings of interest to him, assembled from his writings after his death. It throws more light on Yün Shou-p'ing and the theories and practices of his school than on the paintings discussed.

Chüan 1 contains statements on the theory of painting. Chüan 2 contains discussions of those painters from whom the early Ch'ing orthodox school traced its lineage (Tung Yüan and Chu-jan, Huang Kung-wang and his contemporaries), as well as discussions of the members of the orthodox school of the early Ch'ing (the Four Wangs, etc.). This chüan also contains interesting anecdotal material on certain famous paintings by some of the artists discussed, such as the Fu-ch'un shan-chü t'u by Huang Kung-wang. Chüan 3 consists of descriptions and discussions of specific paintings. Chüan 4 consists of poems about painters and paintings.

49. Kao Shih-ch'i 高士奇, Chiang-ts'un hsiao-hsia lu 江邨銷夏錄. 1693. 3 chüan. (Ferguson, 6, 5). ISSCHC facsimile reprint of the 1923 edition (1970).

Kao Shih-ch'i (1645-1704) was a scholar, collector and a personal secretary to the K'ang-hsi emperor (reigned 1662-1722).

Completed in 1693, Chiang-ts'un hsiao-hsia lu is a catalogue of the better paintings and calligraphy that Kao Shih-ch'i had seen in the three years preceding 1693, each of the three chüan being devoted to the items he saw in one year. Within each chüan, the items are arranged in a chronological order, regardless of their format; paintings and calligraphy are not put into separate categories. They range from the Six Dynasties to the Ming, but exclude works by Tung Ch'i-ch'ang because "they are so important and so numerous that they merit a separate volume". Each entry contains such information as dimensions, materials, description of subject matter, artist's signature, seals and inscriptions, as well as other seals and colophons, including those by Kao Shih-ch'i.

Compared to such earlier catalogues as T'ieh-wang shan-hu (q.v., no. 30) and Ch'ing-ho shu hua fang (q.v.), Kao Shih-ch'i's catalogue contains much fuller information and is more consistent. Compilers of many subsequent catalogues used it as their model, frankly acknowledging their debt to Kao. However, the commendable methodical approach is not matched by an equally high level of connoisseurship as the entries have no critical statements.

50. Kao Shih-ch'i 高士奇, Chiang-ts'un shu hua mu 江村書畫目. 1 chüan. (Ferguson, 6, 4). MSTS, vol. 24, V/8 (under the title of Kao Wen-k'o Kung shu hua chen ying mu 高文恪公書畫真贗目); facsimile reprint of manuscript copy (Hong Kong, 1968). [Freer].

This work is a list of the paintings and calligraphy in the collection of Kao Shih-ch'i (1645-1704) (q.v.). The manuscript copy on which the 1968 reprint is based has a postscript by Wu Hsi-ch'i 吳錫祺 (1746-1818) stating that it was from the hand of Kao Shih-ch'i. But as Lo Chen-yü 羅振玉 (1865-1940) points out in his postscript to the first printed edition (Shanghai, 1924), the manuscript was actually from the hand of a descendant of Kao Shih-ch'i as he is referred to by his posthumous title Wen-k'o 文恪. Another reason why the manuscript was probably by a descendant is that there occur three times the "44th year of the reign of K'ang-hsi", corresponding to 1705, the year after Kao Shih-ch'i's death. It would appear that Chiang-ts'un shu hua mu is a list written by one of Kao's descendants, copied from lists compiled by Kao in his lifetime.

The items number 534, approximately half of which are paintings and half calligraphy. They are divided into nine categories: (1) items to be presented to the emperor; (2) items to be given away as presents; (3) and (4) items without Kao's colophons, to be kept; (5) items of the divine category to be kept forever, calligraphy; (6) ditto, paintings; (7) items of superior quality with colophons by Kao; (8) items for private enjoyment; and (9) works by Tung Ch'i-ch'ang.

Each entry is listed by title, followed by one terse statement as to its authenticity and quality; occasionally an important colophon or title is noted. The price paid for each item is meticulously recorded. It is amusing to observe that the least expensive pieces are in categories (1) and (2). The lists were evidently compiled as personal memoranda and not meant for public consumption.

Despite the terseness of the entries, some of the paintings can be identified with extant works.

51. P'ei-wen-chai shu hua p'u 佩文齋書畫譜.
 1708. 100 chüan. (Ferguson, 8, 1). Undated early edition printed from original blocks. [Freer]. Facsimile reprint of original edition (Taipei, 1969).

On November 24, 1705, the K'ang-hsi emperor (reigned 1662-1722) commissioned Wang Yüan-ch'i 王原祁 (1642-1715) and four other officials to compile a comprehensive work on calligraphy and painting. It was completed in 1708 and was printed under the title P'ei-wen-chai shu hua p'u, with a preface by the emperor.

A vast body of literature was combed for information on calligraphy and painting. The bibliography totals 1,844 titles, some of which were rare books or had not been printed before. In addition to all the available works dealing specifically with calligraphy and painting, the books consulted include classics, histories official, unofficial and local, biographies, many miscellanies, poetry, and even pharmacopoeias.

Forty-two of the 100 chüan are devoted to painting and the rest of the book to calligraphy. These are: chüan 11-18 (discussions of paintings as regards style, method, theory and grading); chüan 21 (emperors and consorts who were painters); chüan 45-58 (biographies of painters); chüan 65-66 (anonymous paintings); chüan 67 (colophons on paintings by the K'ang-hsi emperor); chüan 69 (colophons on paintings by emperors); chüan 81-87 (colophons on paintings by famous people); chüan 90 (the authentication of problematical paintings); and chüan 95-100 (famous collections of paintings).

The parts which Ferguson used for his index are chüan 81-87 and 95-100, and it is with these that we are most concerned. P'ei-wen-chai shu hua p'u is a very valuable anthology in many respects, but it is not the encyclopaedic compilation it set out to be. In the chüan which Ferguson used, the material has been taken from its sources in drastically abbreviated form. This is particularly true of chüan 95-100, where many of the lists of famous collections have been quite arbitrarily reduced. For a full documentation of any painting, the reader is urged to go to the original sources instead of relying on P'ei-wen-chai.

52. Yao Chi-heng 姚際恆, Hao-ku-t'ang shu hua chi 好古堂書畫記. Preface dated 1699. 2 chüan. Supplement, dated 1707. (Ferguson, 6, 1). MSTS, vol. 14, III/8; ISTP, vol. 14, no. 158.

43

Yao Chi-heng (1647-after 1707) was a collector, bibliophile, and an outstanding textual critic of the classics. Hao-ku-t'ang shu hua chi is a catalogue of the calligraphy, paintings and miscellaneous curiosities in his collection, arranged in that order. There are about 100 paintings, ranging from the Five Dynasties to the Ming.

The entries are not standardized and vary a great deal in length. They do not give such catalogue information as measurements and materials, nor do they record all the colophons and seals. Yao Chi-heng selects those colophons and seals which he considers important for recording and discussion. His keenness as a critic is evident in such entries as the one on Tung Yüan's 董源 Hsiao-hsiang t'u 瀟湘圖.

The usefulness of this catalogue is marred by the absence of a table of contents.

53. Chu I-tsun 朱彝尊, P'u-shu-t'ing shu hua pa 曝書亭書畫跋. 1 chüan. (Ferguson, 19, 3). MSTS, vol. 5, I/9; ISTP, vol. 25, no. 202.

Chu I-tsun (1629-1709) was a distinguished historian, antiquarian and poet. P'u-shu-t'ing shu hua pa is a record of the colophons he wrote on 25 paintings and 17 pieces of calligraphy.

The 25 paintings include such important extant works as the Admonitions scroll in the British Museum, the Portrait of the Scholar Fu-sheng in the Municipal Museum in Osaka, and Chao Meng-fu's Autumn Colours in

Ch'iao and Hua Mountains in the Palace Museum in Taiwan. Consequently, this short text is interesting despite its lack of any information other than Chu's colophons.

54. Wu Sheng 吳升, Ta-kuan lu 大觀錄. Prefaces dated 1712. 20 chüan. (Ferguson, 3, 2). ISSCHC facsimile reprint of manuscript copy in the National Central Library (1970).

Wu Sheng's exact dates are not known; he probably died in 1712 or shortly after. According to the preface by Sung Lo 宋犖 (1634-1713) written when he was 79 sui in 1712, Wu Sheng brought the catalogue to him in that year asking for a preface. Another preface, written in the same year by Wang Shih-min's eighth son Wang Shan 王撰 (1645-1728), states that Wu Sheng so exhausted himself writing Ta-kuan lu that he became seriously ill. Wang's preface also records that Wu Sheng was on friendly terms with his father, and no doubt with others of his circle.

Wu Sheng made and kept notes on the paintings and calligraphy he saw, and Ta-kuan lu is an important catalogue. Chüan 1-9 are devoted to calligraphy. Chüan 10 consists of a list of scholar-officials of the Yüan and Ming dynasties, each with a short biography. Chüan 11-20 are devoted to about 450 paintings ranging from the Six Dynasties to the Ming, a considerable number of which can be identified with important extant paintings.

Each entry records the material, technique and dimensions of the painting; it describes its subject matter and style; it transcribes all the inscriptions and colophons; and there are usually critical comments by Wu Sheng. Biographical details of painters are given at the beginning of the entry for the first work by each artist; anecdotes on paintings are sometimes given. Thus, Ta-kuan lu is more informative than most catalogues. There are, however, two omissions: it records hardly any seals, and it does not state in whose collection a painting was at the time Wu Sheng saw it.

The first edition of Ta-kuan lu, collated by Li Tsu-nien 李祖年 from three manuscript copies, was printed in 1920. These three copies contain a number of textual variations. For example, one of them is without the biographies now contained in chüan 10. These biographies seem something of an anomaly as they are only of scholar-officials of the Yüan and Ming. There are two possible explanations for this. One is that Wu Sheng intended to compile a more complete list but died before doing so. The other is that it was compiled by some other person and was somehow incorporated into some of the manuscript copies. The biographies are brief and add little to what we know of the well documented personalities, but they are useful for the less known figures.

55. Li O 厲鶚, Nan-Sung yüan hua lu 南宋院畫錄.
    1721. 8 chüan, supplement 1 chüan. (Ferguson, 9, 2). MSTS, vol. 17, IV/4; ISTP, vol. 15, no. 128.

Li O (1692-1752) was a poet and scholar. Nan-Sung yüan hua lu is a text on the Southern Sung Painting Academy, its artists and their paintings. The compilation is completely made up of quotations from diverse sources, including official history, local histories, painting catalogues, texts on the theory of painting, miscellanies, and so on. The bibliography at the end lists 91 titles and they range from Sung to early Ch'ing in date.

Chüan 1 is an odd collection of 31 quotations on diverse aspects of the Academy. Chüan 2-8 are devoted to 97 artists of the Academy, arranged in a chronological order. Under each artist are assembled quotations on him or particular paintings by him, many in the form of colophons.

Li O used his sources uncritically. Given the array of reference works, a much more intelligible introductory chüan 1 could have been compiled. The merit of this text is that anyone working on any of these 97 Southern Sung Academy artists can use it as a short cut to the information in the 91 works cited in the bibliography.

56. Chou Erh-hsüeh 周二學, I-chüeh pien 一角編.
    Preface dated 1728. 2 chüan. (Ferguson, 1, 1).
    SLTS, tse 11. [Library of Congress].

Chou Erh-hsüeh was a Hangchou collector active in the early 18th century. I-chüeh pien records about 35 paintings and seven pieces of calligraphy in his collection. In his preface, Chou states that only those items in good condition were included. The pieces are arranged in the order in which they were acquired in the years 1712 to 1728.

All the paintings are of the Ming dynasty. Each entry provides full information on the painting: dimensions, materials, description, seals, and transcription of colophons. Furthermore, there is information on the kind of silk used on the mounting and the material of the roller knobs.

Chou Erh-hsüeh was obviously interested in mounting, for he was the author of a treatise on the subject entitled Shang-yen su-hsin lu 賞延素心錄 . For a fuller discussion of Chou Erh-hsüeh, see R.H. van Gulik, Chinese Pictorial Art as Viewed by the Connoisseur (Rome, 1958), p. 315ff.

57. An Ch'i 安岐, Mo-yüan hui-kuan 墨緣彙觀. Preface dated 1742. 4 chüan, supplement 2 chüan. (Ferguson, 15, 4). ISTP, vol. 17, no. 161.

An Ch'i (ca. 1683-after 1744), a wealthy salt merchant of Korean extraction resident in Tientsin, was a distinguished collector and connoisseur. Mo-yüan hui-kuan, which may be paraphrased as "A Record of the Calligraphy and Painting it was my Destiny to See", is an annotated catalogue of the calligraphy and paintings in his collection as well as some of those he saw belonging to others. His preface is dated 1742, but the very first entry in chüan 1 was added in 1744 when he obtained a choice piece of calligraphy.

Chüan 1-2 are devoted to calligraphy, chüan 3-4 to paintings, which range from works attributed to Ku K'ai-chih to those by Tung Ch'i-ch'ang. An Ch'i does not include in his catalogue any paintings by Ch'ing artists, nor does he include any Ch'ing dynasty seals in his entries. One hundred and fifteen handscrolls, hanging scrolls and a small number of albums of single artists are arranged chronologically; these are followed by 14 albums each containing works by more than one artist. For each item, An Ch'i specifies the size, material, technique, and gives a brief description of the subject matter. He records and transcribes all but the least important of the seals and colophons. Critical comments are plentiful, and from these it is evident that An Ch'i was a connoisseur of remarkable insight and discernment. He would question traditional attributions, even those perpetuated by older and more famous connoisseurs, if he felt justified in doing so.

Appended to chüan 2 is a supplement on calligraphy, and likewise appended to chüan 4 is a supplement on paintings which number 122 items. The entries in the supplement are brief, providing little more than a comment or two about seals and inscriptions, and occasionally there are errors. These have given rise to the suggestion that the supplement was written by An Ch'i's son, An Yüan-chung 安元忠, when some of the paintings had been sold after the collector's death and the decline of the family fortune; but this cannot be substantiated.

A number of An Ch'i's paintings and calligraphy were acquired by the Ch'ien-lung emperor in 1746 and are now in the National Palace Museum in Taiwan, and some items found their way into Western collections in the 20th century. Consequently, this important catalogue is of exceptional interest as it can be studied in conjunction with extant paintings.

For a fuller discussion of the catalogue, see Thomas Lawton, "The Mo-yüan hui-kuan by An Ch'i", in National Palace Museum Quarterly, Special Issue No. 1: Symposium in Honor of Dr. Chiang Fu-tsung on his 70th Birthday (Taipei, 1969), pp. 13-35. For a translation of chüan 3-4 and supplement into English, see Thomas Lawton, An Eighteenth Century Chinese Catalogue of Calligraphy and Painting, unpublished Ph.D. dissertation presented to Harvard University, 1970.

58a. Chang Chao 張照 and others, Pi-tien chu-lin 秘殿珠林. 1744. 24 chüan. (Ferguson, 10, 8). Facsimile reprint of an original manuscript copy (Palace Museum, Taipei, 1971). [Freer].

In January, 1744, the Ch'ien-lung emperor commissioned the compilation of a catalogue of the Buddhist and Taoist paintings and texts in the imperial collection. The catalogue was completed and presented to the throne in the summer of the same year. This marked the beginning of a series of catalogues of the Ch'ing imperial collection compiled during the reigns of the Ch'ien-lung (1736-1795) and Chia-ch'ing (1796-1820) emperors.

In his directive to the board of editors, the Ch'ien-lung emperor decreed that the storage location

of the paintings was to serve as the broad basis for
the arrangement of the material to be catalogued.
This principle, of dubious merit, was adhered to in
all the subsequent catalogues, rendering them difficult to use without an index. (This defect is remedied
by the 1971 reprint which has a comprehensive index
prepared by the Palace Museum staff). Within the grouping of the halls or palaces in which the items were
stored, the following order was observed: works by the
Ch'ing emperors, works by noted calligraphers and
painters, and printed texts and images. A distinction
is made between those works which are considered to be
of good quality and those considered to be of secondary
quality, designated "shang-teng 上等" and "tz'u-teng
次等" respectively. For the former, all pertinent
information on materials, technique, measurements, signature, inscriptions, colophons and seals is recorded
and transcribed. For the latter, the information is
much less complete. Only signatures and the names of
the writers of colophons are recorded.

58b. Wang Chieh 王杰 and others, Pi-tien chu-lin
hsü-pien 秘殿珠林續編. 1793. 8 chüan.
(Ferguson, 10, 8). First printed edition, 1948.
Facsimile reprint of an original manuscript copy
(Palace Museum, Taipei, 1971). [Freer].

In 1791, forty-seven years after the completion
of Pi-tien chu-lin (q.v.), a sequel was commissioned
by the Ch'ien-lung emperor and it was completed in 1793.

Pi-tien chu-lin hsü-pien was compiled in conjunction with Shih-ch'ü pao-chi hsü-pien (q.v.) and in both the 1948 and 1971 editions, the two hsü-pien appear under one title. They are similar in organization and contents of individual entries, and their differences from their respective predecessors are also comparable. The remarks on Shih-ch'ü pao-chi hsü-pien apply equally to Pi-tien chu-lin hsü-pien.

58c. Hu Ching 胡敬, Pi-tien chu-lin san-pien 秘殿珠林三編. 1816. 4 chüan. (Ferguson, 10, 8). Facsimile reprint of an original manuscript copy (Palace Museum, Taipei, 1969). [Freer].

The final sequel to Pi-tien chu-lin (q.v.) was compiled by order of the Chia-ch'ing emperor in 1816 in conjunction with Shih-ch'ü pao-chi san-pien (q.v.), and they appear under one title in the 1969 edition. In every respect it is similar to Pi-tien chu-lin hsü-pien (q.v.).

59a. Chang Chao 張照 and others, Shih-ch'ü pao-chi 石渠寶笈. 1745. (Ferguson, 5, 8). HFL facsimile reprint (1918) of the SKCS text; 44 chüan. [Freer]. Facsimile reprint of an original manuscript copy (Palace Museum, Taipei, 1971); 8+8+8+12 chüan, 9 appendices. [Freer].

On April 23, 1744, the Ch'ien-lung emperor commissioned the compilation of a catalogue of the paintings and calligraphy in the imperial collection. Entitled <u>Shih-ch'ü pao-chi</u>, it was completed in 1745 and was formally presented to the throne in the tenth month, corresponding to October 25-November 22, 1745.

The paintings include those items (landscapes, birds and flowers, secular figure paintings, etc.) which were stored in various palaces and halls in Peking. They do not include the Taoist and Buddhist paintings (see <u>Pi-tien chu-lin</u> and sequels, <u>qq.v.</u>), nor the portraits of emperors and meritorious officials (see <u>Nan-hsün-tien tsun-ts'ang t'u-hsiang mu</u> and <u>Ch'a-k'u ts'ang-chu t'u-hsiang mu</u>, <u>qq.v.</u>), nor any of the paintings kept in the summer palaces at Mukden and Jehol (see <u>Sheng-ching ku-kung shu hua lu</u> and <u>Nei-wu-pu ku-wu ch'en-lieh-so hua mu-lu</u>, <u>qq.v.</u>).

As in <u>Pi-tien chu-lin</u>, the material is arranged according to the hall or palace where the paintings and calligraphy were stored. These halls number fourteen, but it is evident that the bulk of the collection was stored in four of them, namely, Ch'ien-ch'ing-kung 乾清宮, Yang-hsin-tien 養心殿, Chung-hua-kung 重華宮, and Yü-shu-fang 御書房. Within the context of each hall, the items are grouped into the following categories: (1) calligraphy in albums, (2) paintings in albums, (3) calligraphy and paintings combined in albums, (4) calligraphy on handscrolls, (5) paintings on handscrolls, (6) calligraphy and paintings combined on handscrolls, (7) calligraphy on hanging scrolls, (8) paintings on hanging scrolls, and (9) calligraphy and paintings combined on hanging scrolls. Within each category works by the Ch'ing emperors (Shun-chih, K'ang-hsi and Ch'ien-lung) are catalogued first, followed by works by calligraphers and painters in chronological sequence. The organization of the material according to storage location renders the catalogue difficult to use. The 1918 edition has neither table of contents nor index, and the only way to use it was through Ferguson. But the 1971 reprint has both a table of contents at the beginning of each chüan and a most comprehensive index which lists all the items under individual painters and calligraphers, as well as all the colophons under their writers.

Again, as in <u>Pi-tien chu-lin</u> (<u>q.v.</u>), all the items in the catalogue are designated either "<u>shang-teng</u> 上等" (superior category) or "<u>tz'u-teng</u> 次等" (secondary category). Entries for the latter are brief. Although these "secondary" items form but a small proportion of the total, they could have been more fully catalogued. The entries for the "superior" items contain full information on dimensions, materials, technique, signature, inscriptions, colophons and seals, written with consistency and meticulous care. The attributions are strictly traditional or according to what the Ch'ien-lung emperor had pronounced on them. Occasionally the compilers would contribute a few comments at the end of an entry, but on the whole, they show little evidence of independent research. This is regrettable but perhaps understandable as the catalogue was commissioned by the emperor whose self-esteem as a connoisseur was enormous.

It will be noticed that the 1918 and 1971 editions are not identical in arrangement. In the 1971 reprint, which is actually based on an earlier text than the 1918 reprint, the chüan are not numbered consecutively, or more precisely, they are numbered consecutively only within each of the four principal halls, while the relatively small number of items in the ten other halls are relegated to the appendices. In some of the entries in the appendices, there are a number of colophons by Ch'ien-lung which post-date 1745, the year of completion of Shih-ch'ü pao-chi. For example, the entry for the Tzu-ming version of the Fu-ch'un shan-chü t'u attributed to Huang Kung-wang includes colophons by the emperor dated in correspondence to 1746, 1747 and 1748 (p. 1244). This anomaly indicates that either the appendices were added after 1745, or the entries were brought up-to-date after the emperor had written more colophons. It would appear that at the time when Shih-ch'ü pao-chi was incorporated into the Ssu-k'u ch'üan-shu in the 1770's and 1780's, certain changes were made to the original text. These are: changes in the order necessitated by changes in the physical location of certain groups of paintings and calligraphy; the appendices were turned into regular chüan; and all the chüan were given consecutive numbers, with designation of hall locations.

59b. Wang Chieh 王杰, and others, Shih-ch'ü pao-chi hsü-pien 石渠寶笈續編. 1793. 85 chüan. (Ferguson, 5, 8). Facsimile reprint of an original manuscript copy (1948). [Freer]. Facsimile reprint of an original manuscript copy (Palace Museum, Taipei, 1971). [Freer].

In 1791, forty-six years after the completion of Shih-ch'ü pao-chi (q.v.), the Ch'ien-lung emperor commissioned a board of ten editors to compile a sequel to that catalogue. Shih-ch'ü pao-chi hsü-pien was completed in 1793 and bears a preface of that date by the emperor. Basically it is a catalogue of the large numbers of calligraphy and paintings amassed by the emperor through gifts from officials and occasionally through purchase in the intervening forty-six years. But it also records a large number of works by Ch'ien-lung himself.

In organization the hsü-pien follows its predecessor, but it has an index in the beginning to works listed under their artists who are arranged in a chrological order. Ironically the index does not serve its purpose well because the references are to names of halls and palaces, of which there are many more than in Shih-ch'ü pao-chi, rather than to pagination. However, with the 1971 reprint, which has a comprehensive index of paintings and colophons with references to normal pagination, the problem has disappeared.

In content, hsü-pien is a better catalogue than its predecessor. The qualitative classification into "superior" and "secondary" categories is abolished, so that all the paintings are catalogued equally fully. Compilers' comments are more frequent than in Shih-ch'ü pao-chi, and these contain much useful information on the identity of the lesser known collectors and connoisseurs who had affixed seals or written colophons on the paintings. If the editors are not as independent in their final evaluation of the artistic worth of the paintings as we would wish, it is because of the nature of the catalogue being commissioned by the emperor. In all but this one respect, Shih-ch'ü pao-chi hsü-pien is an exemplary catalogue.

Several innovations in the lay-out, such as the use of paragraphs, of indenting, and of small characters for the editors' comments, make the catalogue much easier to use and better in appearance than its predecessor.

59c. Hu Ching 胡敬 and others, Shih-ch'ü pao-chi san-pien 石渠寶笈三編 . 1816. (Ferguson, 5, 8). Facsimile reprint of an original manuscript copy (Palace Museum, Taipei, 1969). 4618 pp. [Freer].

In 1816, an inventory was taken of the imperial collection of painting and calligraphy, and it was found that some 2,000 more items had been added to the collection since the completion of Shih-ch'ü pao-chi hsü-pien and Pi-tien chu-lin hsü-pien (qq.v.) in 1793. The Chia-ch'ing emperor therefore commissioned the compilation of a further sequel to the catalogues.

In organization, method and content of individual entries, and in lay-out, Shih-ch'ü pao-chi san-pien closely resembles hsü-pien and most of the remarks on hsü-pien apply. One difference is that, unlike in hsü-pien, the component parts of the catalogue are not numbered consecutively, so that it is not possible to cite the number of chüan, and the number of pages in the

1969 reprint is given instead.

Shih-ch'ü pao-chi san-pien includes a section (pp. 4514-4618) on the portraits of past emperors, empresses, sages and meritorious officials stored in the Nan-hsün-tien. It is actually a combined list of the items recorded in Nan-hsün-tien tsun-ts'ang t'u-hsiang mu and in Ch'a-k'u ts'ang-chu t'u-hsiang mu (qq.v.). The number of hanging scrolls, albums and handscrolls totals 121, which agrees exactly with the figures in the two earlier texts. However, the entries are much fuller than in the earlier texts. Apart from giving the dimensions and noting the materials used, each entry describes the costume of the sitter and provides lengthy biographical information. This section of san-pien is sometimes treated as an independent text under the title of Nan-hsün-tien t'u-hsiang k'ao 南薰殿圖像考, and has been printed as such in a collection of Hu Ching's writings.

The importance of all three parts of Shih-ch'ü pao-chi can hardly be exaggerated. They are important because the paintings were what they were, and because a large proportion have survived and are available for study in the Palace Museum in Taiwan, and a small number are in public and private collections elsewhere.

60. Nan-hsün-tien tsun-ts'ang t'u-hsiang mu 南薰殿尊藏圖像目. 1749. 1 chüan. (Ferguson, 9, 5). SLTS. [Library of Congress].

This is an inventory, taken in 1749 by order of the Ch'ien-lung emperor, of the portraits of past emperors and empresses stored in the Nan-hsün-tien. The 79 hanging scrolls, 15 albums and three handscrolls are arranged in a chronological order of the subjects of the portraits, beginning with the rulers of the legendary dynasties through to the Ming. For each portrait, the dimensions are given and the materials noted.

The bulk of these portraits (67 hanging scrolls, ten albums and two handscrolls) are preserved in the Palace Museum in Taiwan, and are recorded in Ku-kung shu hua lu (q.v.), chüan 7.

61. <u>Ch'a-k'u ts'ang-chu t'u-hsiang mu</u> 茶庫藏貯圖像目. 1749. 1 <u>chüan</u>. (Ferguson, 10, 9). SLTS. [Library of Congress].

This is an inventory, taken in 1749 by order of the Ch'ien-lung emperor, of the portraits of meritorious officials stored in the Ch'a-k'u. (The Ch'a-k'u, or Tea Storehouse, was one of the six imperial storehouses administered by the Kuang-ch'u-ssu 廣儲司, Department of Supplies. It would seem that even the Ch'ien-lung emperor had storage problems.)

The 21 hanging scrolls and three albums are arranged in a chronological order of the subjects of the portraits, from Han to T'ang. For each portrait, the dimensions are given and the materials noted.

62. Ch'en Chuan 陳撰, <u>Yü-chi-shan-fang hua wai-lu</u> 玉几山房畫外錄. 2 chüan. (Ferguson, 5, 4). MSTS, vol. 4, I/8; ISTP, vol. 14, no. 125.

Ch'en Chuan was a poet and painter of landscape and flowers who lived approximately from 1670 to 1740. <u>Yü-chi-shan-fang hua wai-lu</u> is a compilation of quotations on paintings chosen at random from the writings of 49 persons of the late Ming and early Ch'ing. The value of this text is minimal.

63. Tu Mu 都穆 [sic., Anon.], <u>T'ieh-wang shan-hu</u> 鐵網珊瑚. 20 chüan. (Ferguson, 20, 2). ISSCHC facsimile reprint of the manuscript copy in the National Central Library (1970).

The traditional attribution of this text to Tu Mu (1458-1525) is incorrect. The edition cited above has no preface, but some editions of <u>T'ieh-wang shan-hu</u> have a preface by Shen Te-ch'ien 沈德潛 (1673-1769) dated 1758. In it, Shen attributes the work to Tu Mu and states that he was asked to contribute a preface by Tu's seventh generation descendant Tu Chao-pin 都肇斌 who was instrumental in arranging to have the text printed for the first time. <u>T'ieh-wang shan-hu</u> is probably a fabrication of the Ch'ieh-lung period.

The text is a hopeless hotch-potch made up of various corrupt texts on painting, calligraphy, bronzes, musical instruments, and so on, arranged in a most haphazard way. About half the <u>chüan</u> are devoted to painting. These are: <u>chüan</u> 4 to the beginning of <u>chüan</u> 8;

chüan 12 to the first half of chüan 15; and chüan 18-
20. One of the texts on painting included is Tu Mu's
Yü-i pien (q.v.), and this may account for the persis-
tent misattribution of the entire T'ieh-wang shan-hu
to him. It occupies chüan 5.

Other texts on painting incorporated are Ho Liang-
chün's "Shu hua ming-hsin lu" (q.v.) in chüan 6:15a-22b;
T'ang Hou's Hua chien (q.v.) in chüan 12; T'ang Yün-mou's
Yün-yen kuo-yen hsü-lu (q.v.) in chüan 14; and Chou Mi's
Yün-yen kuo-yen lu (q.v.) in chüan 18-20. Some of the
other chüan on painting in T'ieh-wang shan-hu are of
uncertain authorship.

That T'ieh-wang shan-hu is a compilation post-
dating Tu Mu's death in 1525 is a matter of absolute
certainty. Lo Liang-chün's "Shu hua ming-hsin lu" has
a preface dated 1556 and a postscript dated 1567. There
are other references in the text to dates after 1525
(chüan 7:17b; chüan 8:4a).

It is evident that T'ieh-wang shan-hu does not
deserve any serious attention.

64. Chang Keng 張庚 , T'u-hua ching-i shih 圖畫
精意識 . 1 chüan. (Ferguson, 14, 2). MSTS,
vol. 11, III/2; ISTP, vol. 14, no. 121.

Chang Keng (1685-1760) was the compiler of several
books on Ch'ing painters. T'u-hua ching-i shih records
85 paintings which he had seen. The text was not printed
until the late 19th century; it has a preface dated 1888.

The 85 paintings range from the T'ang to Ming, and a number of them are important paintings. The text is not a catalogue in the strict sense of the word. The items are not arranged in chronological order, nor do the entries contain all the pertinent information such as measurements and a complete transcription of all the colophons and seals. What the work lacks in completeness it makes up for in its stylistic analysis of some of the paintings. The discussions of stylistic matters are sound, and they are all the more valuable for being so rare in Chinese texts.

65. Ch'en Ch'uo 陳焯, Hsiang-kuan-chai yü-shang pien 湘館齋寓賞編. Preface dated 1762. 6 chüan. (Ferguson, 12, 2). MSTS, vol. 19, IV/8; ISTP, vol. 19, no. 169.

Ch'en Ch'uo was a scholar and connoisseur active in the reign of Ch'ien-lung in the 18th century. Hsiang-kuan-chai yü-shang pien is a catalogue of the calligraphy and paintings he had seen. Chüan 1-4 are devoted to calligraphy, and chüan 5-6 to 73 paintings ranging from the Sung to the Ming, and arranged chronologically. None of the paintings is of any particular importance. Each entry gives materials and dimensions and records inscriptions, colophons and seals. Ch'en usually records the dates and the circumstances under which he saw the paintings. His comments are in the nature of appreciation rather than research and critical judgement.

66. Lu Shih-hua 陸時化, <u>Wu-Yüeh so-chien shu hua lu 吳越所見書畫錄</u>. Preface dated 1776. 6 chüan. (Ferguson, 7, 2). ISSCHC facsimile reprint of the 1909 edition (1972).

Lu Shih-hua (1714-1779) was a connoisseur and <u>Wu-Yüeh so-chien shu hua lu</u> is a catalogue of 628 paintings and calligraphy he saw in his native Suchou and vicinity.

There is no attempt to arrange the material in any systematic way. Paintings and calligraphy are not separated, nor are the different formats of handscroll, hanging scroll and album. Each of the first five chüan records paintings and calligraphy of different dynasties and formats, but within each chüan, the items are in a roughly chronological order. Chüan 6 is devoted to paintings of the Ch'ing dynasty, restricted to the so-called Orthodox School (the Four Wangs, Wu Li and Yün Shou-p'ing).

The individual entries are thorough and written with care. Each entry records the precise measurements of painting and end-papers and gives a description of the painting. Inscriptions, colophons and seals are meticulously transcribed. Occasionally there are biographical details and critical comments.

67. Li Tiao-yüan 李調元, <u>Chu-chia ts'ang-hua pu 諸家藏畫簿</u>. Preface 1778. 10 chüan. (Ferguson, 16, 2). HH. [Freer].

Li Tiao-yüan (1734-1803) was a scholar and bibliophile. Chu-chia ts'ang-hua pu is a list of the titles of paintings in various collections in the past, copied verbatim from the first five-sixths of chüan 2 of Shih-ku-t'ang shu hua hui-k'ao (q.v.) by Pien Yung-yü.

68. Juan Yüan 阮元 , Shih-ch'ü sui-pi 石渠隨筆.
8 chüan. (Ferguson, 5, 7). Yangchou, n.d.
[Freer].

Juan Yüan (1764-1849), the celebrated antiquarian and bibliophile, was one of the ten editors of Shih-ch'ü pao-chi hsü-pien and Pi-tien chu-lin hsü-pien (qq.v.). While compiling these catalogues in the years 1791-93, he made notes on some of the paintings and calligraphy, and these notes were published for the first time in 1842 under the title Shih-ch'ü sui-pi.

The discussions of various paintings and calligraphy follow no fixed form, but vary in length according to the intrinsic interest of each. They testify to the keenness of Juan Yüan's mind and the independence of his approach to the problems of connoisseurship. These qualities were all the more remarkable as he was only in his twenties when the notes were compiled. Informal in its arrangement and full of lively observations, this text is an admirable companion and the perfect counterfoil to the official Shih-ch'ü pao-chi hsü-pien.

69. Shih-pai-chai chu-jen 十百齋主人, <u>Shih-pai-chai shu hua lu</u> 十百齋書畫錄. 22 chüan. (Ferguson, 2, 1). Undated manuscript copy. [Stanford University Art Library].

The identity of the compiler remains a mystery. The short preface, unsigned and undated, states that the master of Shih-pai-chai had seen countless paintings and calligraphy, and had a collection of considerable size. It further states that <u>Shih-pai-chai shu hua lu</u> was compiled over a period of twenty years.

In the text, no distinction is made between the items owned by the compiler and those belonging to others, if indeed it included things in his collection. More than a thousand paintings and calligraphy are recorded, the earliest items bearing a most improbable Han attribution. A fair number bear Sung and Yüan attributions, and the most numerous are Ming. The latest pieces are by painters active in the latter half of the 18th century, and a very tentative date around 1800 is advanced for the text.

The paintings and calligraphy are not separated, nor are they arranged according to format. There is no overall chronological sequence but within each <u>chüan</u> the items are in a more or less chronological order. This suggests that the whole catalogue may indeed have been compiled over 20 years, with the individual <u>chüan</u> organized and written up after a certain interval of time.

Each entry records dimensions and materials; it records the artist's signature and inscriptions as well as colophons by and seals of important people. There

are no critical comments or research of any sort. As
far as can be judged from the text, the paintings are
of indifferent quality. In the Stanford text, there
is a single character at the top of each entry grading
the item as either "excellent", "good", "ordinary", or
"suspicious".

<u>Shih-pai-chai shu hua lu</u> appears to have never
been printed. Ferguson used a manuscript copy, and
the text here cited is also in manuscript form.

70. Wang Wen-chih 王文治, <u>K'uai-yü-t'ang t'i-pa</u>
快雨堂題跋. 8 <u>chüan</u>. (Ferguson, 7, 4).
n.d. [Harvard-Yenching].

Wang Wen-chih (1730-1802) was a poet and calligrapher of the Ch'ien-lung period. <u>K'uai-yü-t'ang
t'i-pa</u>, compiled by a pupil probably after Wang Wen-
chih's death, is a collection of his colophons on some
of the calligraphy and paintings he saw. <u>Chüan</u> 1-6
are devoted to calligraphy and <u>chüan</u> 7 and 8 to fifty
paintings, ranging from Sung to Ch'ing. The paintings
are arranged chronologically regardless of format.

Being colophons, the entries do not include any
physical data such as materials, measurements and
seals. They contain interesting critical comments
and are informative on the transmission of the paintings. Occasionally Wang Wen-chih would transcribe an
earlier colophon.

It is regrettable that the colophons here collected represent only a portion of Wang Wen-chih's

writings in this area. Among the omissions are his colophons on such important extant paintings as Li Shan's <u>Wind and Snow in the Fir-pines</u> and Ch'iu Ying's <u>Landscape in the Style of Li T'ang</u>. Presumably the pupil who compiled the text did not have access to all the pertinent material.

71. Ch'ing-fou-shan-jen 青浮山人, <u>Tung Hua-t'ing shu hua lu</u> 董華庭書畫錄. 1 <u>chüan</u>. (Ferguson, 13, 3). ISTP, vol. 25, no. 192.

Ch'ing-fou-shan-jen has not been identified; he lived in the Ch'ing dynasty. <u>Tung Hua-t'ing shu hua lu</u> is a catalogue of some of Tung Ch'i-ch'ang's works. They consist of: (1) handscrolls: 9 paintings and 16 calligraphy; (2) hanging scrolls: 21 paintings and 5 calligraphy; and (3) albums: 9 paintings and 21 calligraphy.

For each item, Ch'ing-fou-shan-jen gives the title, the materials, the dimensions and transcribes Tung Ch'i-ch'ang's inscriptions and seals. In some cases, there are colophons by and seals of other people, some of whom were contemporaries of Tung Ch'i-ch'ang, others were later collectors and connoisseurs. The latest colophon appears to be one by Wang Wen-chih 王文治 (1730-1802) dated 1800, which indicates that the text is a 19th century compilation. There is no preface to inform the reader whether the paintings and calligraphy were actually seen by the compiler or were merely recorded in other texts.

72. Hu Ching 胡敬, Hsi-Ch'ing cha chi 西清劄記.
    1816. 4 chüan. (Ferguson, 6, 8). ISSCHC facsimile reprint of the 1816 edition (1970).

Hsi-Ch'ing cha chi consists of notes on various paintings and calligraphy Hu Ching examined and catalogued when preparing Shih-ch'ü pao-chi san-pien (q.v.), the final sequel to the catalogue of the Ch'ing imperial collection. It is comparable to Juan Yüan's Shih-ch'ü sui-pi (q.v.).

All the entries are dated, and they are arranged according to the date on which Hu Ching saw the items. The choices were probably made on the basis of quality, as there are no more than one or two items for each day. The entries give fairly detailed descriptions of the paintings, record some colophons and usually end with a paragraph of comments consisting of the results of Hu Ching's own research. This text is a useful addition to san-pien.

73. Hu Ching 胡敬, Kuo-ch'ao yüan hua lu 國朝院畫錄. 1816. 2 chüan. (Ferguson, 11, 1). ISSCHC facsimile reprint of the 1816 edition (1970).

Hu Ching was the chief editor of Shih-ch'ü pao-chi san-pien (q.v.). Kuo-ch'ao yüan hua lu deals with 53 court painters of the Ch'ing dynasty up to the early 19th century. For each artist, there is a very brief biography running no more than one line, followed by a list of his paintings recorded in Shih-

ch'ü pao-chi as well as in its hsü-pien and san-pien
(qq.v.). In many cases, the paintings are listed by
title only. In others, Hu Ching has added annotations
noting any colophons added by the Ch'ien-lung emperor,
sometimes transcribing the verses.

Although this text is nothing more than excerpts
from the three parts of Shih-ch'ü pao-chi, its one
merit is that it isolates the Ch'ing court painters
from all the other painters recorded in those catalogues, presenting them as a group with their status
as court painters in common. Anyone interested in
pursuing them further can go to the fuller sources
(Shih-ch'ü pao-chi and Ku-kung shu hua lu, qq.v.)
as well as to Pi-tien chu-lin and its supplements
(qq.v.) where some of their works are recorded.

74. Wu Hsiu 吳修, Ch'ing-hsia-kuan lun-hua chüeh-
chü 青霞館論畫絕句. Preface dated 1824.
1 chüan. (Ferguson, 8, 6). MSTS, vol. 8, II/6;
ISTP, vol. 16, no. 139.

Wu Hsiu (1764-1827) was a scholar and painter.
Ch'ing-hsia-kuan lun-hua chüeh-chü is an assemblage
of 100 poems about 100 paintings Wu Hsiu had seen,
ranging from the T'ang to the Ch'ing dynasty. Some
of these were in his own collection, and others belonged to friends.

The poems are of the chüeh-chü type, consisting
of four lines with seven characters to each line. They
are not at all informative. However, following each
poem is a paragraph in prose whose style is informal

and chatty, containing such data as dimensions, materials, subject matter, colophons, and references to earlier catalogues, although not as fully or consistently as one would wish. In addition, Wu Hsiu would relate the circumstances under which he acquired a painting, or, if a painting belonged to someone else, he would give the name of the current owner. In a few instances, he includes interesting information on recent mountings which the paintings had undergone. Some of the paintings recorded in this text are extant.

75. P'an Shih-huang 潘世璜, <u>Hsü-ching-chai yün-yen kuo-yen lu</u> 須靜齋雲烟過眼錄. 1 chüan. (Ferguson, 12, 13). MSTS, vol. 7, II/4; ISTP, vol. 18, no. 162.

P'an Shih-huang (1764-1829) belonged to a family of distinguished scholars. <u>Hsü-ching-chai yün-yen kuo-yen lu</u> is a record of the calligraphy and paintings shown to him by relatives and friends between the years 1804 and 1829. The preface by his grandson P'an Tsun-ch'i 潘遵祁 is dated 1855. The text was printed in 1910 with a postscript bearing that date.

The paintings are few in number and insignificant. The entries are arranged in the order in which P'an Shih-huang saw them. They do not record measurements and materials; inscriptions and colophons are noted but not transcribed. Occasionally there are comments by the compiler. Appended to certain entries are terse statements by Ku Wen-pin 顧文彬 (1811-1889) (<u>q.v.</u>) and Fei Nien-tz'u 費念慈 (1855-1905). The value of this text is minimal.

76. Chang Ta-yung 張大鏞, <u>Tzu-i-yüeh-chai shu hua lu</u> 自怡悅齋書畫錄. Preface dated 1832. 30 <u>chüan</u>. (Ferguson, 6, 6). [Stanford University Art Library].

<u>Tzu-i-yüeh-chai shu hua lu</u> is a catalogue of more than 500 paintings and calligraphy, the majority of which were in the collection of Chang Ta-yung. The earliest painting bears a Sung attribution, but most of the paintings are of Ch'ing date and a number are by some of Chang's virtually unknown contemporaries.

Paintings and calligraphy are not separated. The items are divided according to format, and within this grouping there is a chronological sequence. Each entry gives the dimensions and notes the materials; it records seals and colophons. There are no critical comments, or references to earlier catalogues.

Chang Ta-yung seems utterly devoid of flexibility in his approach to his catalogue. One piece of calligraphy attributed to Chu Yün-ming is the text of <u>Ko-ku yao-lun</u> 格古要論, the well-known early Ming treatise on antiquities by Ts'ao Chao 曹昭. In the entry for this item, the entire text of this celebrated and easily accessible book is transcribed. The result is a most tedious catalogue, particularly as the paintings are of such mediocre quality.

77. T'ao Liang 陶樑, Hung-tou-shu-kuan shu hua chi 紅豆樹館書畫記. Preface dated 1836. 8 chüan. (Ferguson, 9, 10). ISSCHC facsimile reprint of the 1882 edition (1972).

T'ao Liang (1772-1857) was a collector and Hanlin scholar. Hung-tou-shu-kuan shu hua chi is a catalogue of the more than 300 paintings and calligraphy in his collection; chüan 8 records some paintings and calligraphy which he saw in other people's collections. His preface bears the date of 1836, but the work was not printed until 1882.

The paintings and calligraphy are not put into separate categories, but are arranged together in a chronological sequence. Handscrolls and hanging scrolls are treated together, but albums are grouped together in chüan 6 and 7. Eighteen scrolls and three albums bear pre-Ming attributions, and the remaining paintings are of Ming and Ch'ing date. Each entry gives dimensions, materials and a description of the painting; inscriptions, colophons and seals are fully transcribed. T'ao Liang's remarks provide substantial evidence of his research and sound judgement. In chüan 8, information on current ownership is usually given.

Hung-tou-shu-kuan shu hua chi is typical of the kind of solid catalogue which had become standard by the 19th century.

78. Hu Chi-t'ang 胡積堂, Pi-hsiao-hsüan shu hua lu 筆嘯軒書畫錄. Preface 1839. 2 chüan. (Ferguson, 12, 7). [Stanford University Art Library].

According to the preface by the compiler's friend Wang Tse 王澤, dated 1839, the paintings and calligraphy recorded in Pi-hsiao-hsüan shu hua lu were in Hu Chi-t'ang's own collection.

Chüan 1 records about 320 paintings and calligraphy in the form of hanging scrolls; chüan 2 records a large number of albums, followed by a small number of handscrolls. With a few exceptions, the works are of Ming and Ch'ing date. The entries are brief, recording materials, artists' signatures, inscriptions and seals, and occasionally other people's colophons. Measurements are not given. There are no critical comments and no references to records in earlier texts.

As far as can be judged, the paintings are of indifferent quality, and the catalogue is insignificant.

79. Sun Hsing-yen 孫星衍, P'ing-chin-kuan chien-ts'ang shu hua chi 平津館鑑藏書畫記. 1841. 1 chüan. (Ferguson, 5, 3). GMS, no. 147. [Freer microfilm].

Sun Hsing-yen (1753-1818) was a scholar, bibliophile and calligrapher. P'ing-chin-kuan chien-ts'ang shu hua chi, printed in 1841, was edited by Ch'en Tsung-i 陳宗彝 who discovered the manuscript when he was going through Sun's papers in connection with another publication project. Ch'en's preface is dated 1840.

The catalogue records 60 paintings and some calligraphy, the majority of which were in Sun Hsing-yen's collection while a few belonged to friends. In the case of the latter, Sun would note the current owner. The paintings range from the T'ang to the Ming, the very first entry being the <u>Portraits of Thirteen Emperors</u> attributed to Yen Li-pen now in the Museum of Fine Arts, Boston.

The entries do not give dimensions, information on materials, or description of the paintings. For such a late catalogue, these omissions are unusual. The entries do record seals and transcribe inscriptions and colophons. Sun Hsing-yen did a considerable amount of research on the paintings, and his critical comments are interesting. At the end of the catalogue is a list of 52 titles of paintings with no catalogue information.

80. Wu Jung-kuang 吳榮光, <u>Hsin-ch'ou hsiao-hsia chi</u> 辛丑銷夏記. 1841. 5 <u>chüan</u>. (Ferguson, 7, 5). ISSCHC facsimile reprint of the 1905 edition (1970).

Wu Jung-kuang (1773-1843) was a scholar, collector and official who served in various capacities until the spring of 1841 when he was forced by the emperor to retire. In the summer of that, the <u>hsin-ch'ou</u>, year, he compiled the catalogue <u>Hsin-ch'ou hsiao-hsia chi</u>. It records 144 paintings and calligraphy, some of which were in his own collection and others he had seen.

The 86 pieces of calligraphy and 58 paintings are not put into separate categories; they are arranged chronologically regardless of their format. The earliest paintings have attributions to the Five Dynasties and the latest are late Ming in date. Each entry gives information on materials, measurements and subject matter, and transcribes inscriptions, colophons and seals. In his preface, Wu Jung-kuang states that he takes as his models Sun Ch'eng-tse's Keng-tzu hsiao-hsia chi and Kao Shih-ch'i's Chiang-ts'un hsiao-hsia lu (qq.v.). Actually, his catalogue provides much fuller information on the paintings than the former, and surpasses the latter in research and connoisseurship. The substance of Wu Jung-kuang's comments on the paintings is always interesting. This is an excellent catalogue.

81. Liang Chang-chü 梁章鉅, T'ui-an so-ts'ang chin-shih shu hua pa 退盦所藏金石書畫跋. Preface dated 1845. 20 chüan. (Ferguson, 10, 10). ISSCHC facsimile reprint of the 1845 edition (1972).

Liang Chang-chü (1775-1849) was a scholar, collector and official whose last appointment before retirement was the governorship of Kiangsu province. T'ui-an so-ts'ang chin-shih shu hua pa is a catalogue of the calligraphy, paintings, bronzes and other objects in his collection.

Chüan 11-20 are devoted to paintings, arranged chronologically regardless of format. The earliest have T'ang attributions and the latest are early Ch'ing in date. Most entries give a brief biographical sketch of the artist, and are informative on the history of the painting's transmission. On the other hand, they seldom give such information as dimensions or materials, and only those colophons by eminent collectors are recorded.

82. Chang T'ing-chi 張廷濟, Ch'ing-i-ko t'i-pa 清儀閣題跋. 1 chüan. (Ferguson, 11, 5). [Harvard-Yenching].

Chang T'ing-chi (1768-1848) was an antiquarian and collector. Ch'ing-i-ko t'i-pa is a collection of his study notes on diverse antiquities, including bronze inscriptions, old coins, tiles, stelae and calligraphy. Only five of the entries are concerned with paintings, none of them of significance. The text was edited and printed posthumously in 1892.

83. Chiang Kuang-hsü 蔣光煦, Pieh-hsia-chai shu hua lu 別下齋書畫錄. 7 chüan. (Ferguson, 7, 1). [University of Chicago Library].

Chiang Kuang-hsü (1813-1860) was a noted bibliophile and a collector of painting and calligraphy. Pieh-hsia-chai shu hua lu is a catalogue of his collection, compiled in 1850. In 1859, the Taiping rebels burnt and pillaged his home town of Chia-shih 硤石 in Chekiang province, and most of his collection and his immense library were destroyed. After his death, the surviving manuscript was prepared for publication by his friend Kuan T'ing-fen 管庭芬 (1797-1880), who contributed a preface dated 1865.

The paintings and calligraphy are arranged in no perceivable order, neither chronological nor according to format. The entries contain full information on dimensions, materials, seals, inscriptions and colophons. The collection appears to have been of mediocre quality, and since the paintings no longer exist, the catalogue has little worth except as a record of Chiang Kuang-hsü's collection.

84. Han T'ai-hua 韓泰華, <u>Yü-yü-t'ang shu hua chi</u> 玉雨堂書畫記. Preface dated 1851. 4 <u>chüan</u>. (Ferguson, 5, 5). MSTS, vol. 7, II/3; ISTP, vol. 18, no. 163.

Han T'ai-hua's dates do not appear to be recorded, but he must have been active in the second quarter of the 19th century. The preface by Shen T'ao 沈濤 is dated 1851. <u>Yü-yü-t'ang shu hua chi</u> is the catalogue of a selection of the better pieces from his collection; they number 52 paintings and 28 pieces of calligraphy. The paintings range from Sung to the early Ch'ing.

Dimensions of the paintings are given very infrequently, and as a rule, only the artist's own inscriptions and seals are recorded. On the other hand, Han T'ai-hua is meticulous in giving information on material, subject matter, style and general impressions of the paintings. His statements on his own reaction to the paintings are interesting and suggest that he was a keen connoisseur. Despite the omissions, the catalogue is good, and some of the paintings may be extant.

85. K'ung Kuang-t'ao 孔廣陶, <u>Yüeh-hsüeh-lou shu hua lu</u> 嶽雪樓書畫錄. 1861. 5 <u>chüan</u>. (Ferguson, 17, 1). ISSCHC facsimile reprint of the 1889 edition (1972).

K'ung Kuang-t'ao, active during the middle decades of the 19th century, was a 70th-generation descendant of Confucius. Yüeh-hsüeh-lou shu hua lu is a catalogue of the paintings and calligraphy in his collection. His father K'ung Ch'ih-t'ing 孔熾庭 was a keen collector, and both K'ung Kuang-t'ao and his brother K'ung Kuang-yung 孔廣鏞 (born 1816) became collectors and connoisseurs in their own right.

The 139 items are arranged chronologically. The majority are paintings, ranging from T'ang to Ming. In each entry, K'ung Kuang-t'ao records the material, the dimensions, and the technique of execution. He transcribes all the inscriptions and colophons, including his own, as well as all the seals. His research and critical comments are embodied in his colophons. The entries are of uniform excellence, and some of the paintings are extant.

86. Li Tso-hsien 李佐賢, Shu hua chien-ying 書畫鑑影. 1871. 24 chüan. (Ferguson, 10, 5). ISSCHC facsimile reprint of the 1871 edition (1970).

Li Tso-hsien (chin-shih 1835) was a collector and connoisseur active in the mid-19th century. Shu hua chien-ying is a catalogue of more than 500 paintings and calligraphy which he had seen. The paintings range from T'ang to Ch'ing. They are not separated from the calligraphy, but are organized according to their format of handscrolls, albums and hanging scrolls; within each category, there is a chronological sequence.

Each entry gives full information on dimensions, material and subject matter, and records and transcribes all seals, inscriptions and colophons. In these respects, Shu hua chien-ying is typical of the many excellent catalogues of the 19th century. There are, however, no critical comments by Li Tso-hsien. Some of the paintings recorded are extant.

87. Fang Chün-i 方濬頤, Meng-yüan shu hua lu 夢園書畫錄. Preface dated 1875. 25 chüan. (Ferguson, 14, 3). 1877 edition. [Freer].

Fang Chün-i (1815-1889) was a collector and official who served, among other posts, as salt controller of Kuangtung province, and many of his early acquisitions were from well-known collections in that province. Meng-yüan shu hua lu is a catalogue of about 400 paintings and calligraphy in his collection.

Paintings and calligraphy are not treated separately but are arranged together in chronological sequence regardless of format. The paintings range from the Six Dynasties to the Ch'ing. Each entry gives dimensions, materials and a detailed description of the painting. It records seals and transcribes colophons, including those by Fang Chün-i himself in which his comments on the paintings are to be found. This is a good catalogue and some of the paintings may be extant.

88. Tu Jui-lien 杜瑞聯, <u>Ku-fen-ko shu hua chi</u> 古芬閣書畫記. Preface dated 1881. 18 <u>chüan</u>. (Ferguson, 5, 1). [Library of Congress].

<u>Ku-fen-ko shu hua chi</u> is a catalogue of the paintings and calligraphy in the collection of Tu Jui-lien, who served as inspector of Kueichou province. The collection was large, and many of the works are of improbable antiquity. In painting, the array of Six Dynasties and T'ang works would have been most impressive if they were genuine. This is an indication of the low level of Tu Jui-lien's connoisseurship and calls for caution in accepting even the works of more recent date recorded in the catalogue.

<u>Chüan</u> 9-18 are devoted to painting. Each entry gives measurements and materials, describes the subject matter, and records seals. It also contains a paragraph of comments and encomium.

Much of the text recurs in <u>Yen-fu pien</u> by Yang En-shou (<u>q.v.</u>), who also contributed a preface to <u>Ku-fen-ko shu hua chi</u>, and it is possible that he did some of the writing for Tu Jui-lien.

89. Ko Chin-lang 葛金烺, <u>Ai-jih-yin-lou shu hua lu</u> 愛日吟樓書畫錄. Preface 1881. 4 <u>chüan</u>. (Ferguson, 13, 1). 1910 edition. [Freer]. Ko Ssu-t'ung 葛嗣浵, <u>pu-lu</u> 補錄, 1912, 1 <u>chüan</u>; <u>hsü-lu</u> 續錄, 1913, 8 <u>chüan</u>; <u>pieh-lu</u> 別錄, 1913, 4 <u>chüan</u>. 1913 edition. [Library of Congress].

Ko Chin-lang (died 1890) was a collector active in the late 19th century. Ai-jih-yin-lou shu hua lu is a catalogue of about 110 selected paintings and calligraphy from his collection. They are not put into separate categories, but are arranged in chronological sequence regardless of format. The paintings range from Sung to Ch'ing.

Each entry gives dimensions and information on materials, and transcribes seals, inscriptions and colophons. In addition, there is a paragraph describing the painting, recording its condition and occasionally the price paid for it. It also notes where the painting had been previously recorded, and incorporates some research on the painter and/or some of the personalities whose calligraphy or seals appear on the painting. This is a good and full catalogue, typical of the 19th century.

Ko Chin-lang's son, Ko Ssu-t'ung, subsequently added a supplement of 1 chüan, a sequel of 8 chüan, and an appendix of 4 chüan in which more paintings and calligraphy are recorded in the same manner. However, he appears to be less of a scholar and connoisseur than his father.

90. Ku Wen-pin 顧文彬, Kuo-yün-lou shu hua chi 過雲樓書畫記. Preface 1882. 10 chüan. (Ferguson, 13, 4). ISSCHC facsimile reprint of the 1883 edition (1970).

Ku Wen-pin (1811-1889) was a scholar, calligrapher and collector. Kuo-yün-lou shu hua chi, named after his residence in Suchou which still stands today, is a catalogue of about 200 paintings and some calligraphy in his collection.

In his preface, Ku Wen-pin stated the rules which he set himself for the compilation of the catalogue. Some of them may strike the reader as eccentric. For example, Mi Fei was quoted as saying that the spirit of a painting is lost from silk after 800 years, and for that reason Ku Wen-pin decided to exclude all paintings on silk from his catalogue. Most of the other rules are eminently sound, and they testify to the high level of his connoisseurship. Ku scrupulously excluded all works from his catalogue which he considered spurious, even though they might have been accepted as genuine by earlier connoisseurs.

Chüan 5-10 are devoted to paintings, which range from T'ang to Ch'ing. The catalogue is not very complete on basic data. The entries do describe the paintings but do not give measurements. Seals and colophons are not exhaustively recorded. On the other hand, the catalogue is excellent on background material on artists and paintings, and each entry is the result of thorough research.

Ku Wen-pin's sons and grandsons inherited not only his collection but also his passionate interest in painting and calligraphy, and some of them became quite notable artists. Despite the splitting of the collection, a portion of Ku Wen-pin's original collection has survived. Before his death in 1951, Ku Wen-pin's grandson Ku Kung-hsiung 顧公雄 expressed the wish to present his collection to the nation. By 1961, the entire collection totalling 393 items had been presented by his family to the People's Republic of China. (Lin Ch'iao-mu 林喬木, "Kuo-yün-lou ming-chung Chiang-nan 過雲樓名重江南", in I-lin ts'ung-lu 藝林叢錄, second series, [Hong Kong, 1962]).

91. Yang En-shou 楊恩壽, Yen-fu pien 眼福編. Preface dated 1885. First series, 14 chüan; second series, 15 chüan; third series, 7 chüan. (Ferguson, 11, 6). 1885 edition. [Freer].

Yang En-shou was a close associate of Tu Jui-lien, whose collection of paintings and calligraphy is catalogued in Ku-fen-ko shu hua chi (q.v.).

In his preface to Yen-fu pien, Yang En-shou relates that Tu used to ask him to write colophons on his paintings and calligraphy, and the 14 chüan in the first series record these colophons. This part of the text is worthless because of the dubious quality of Tu Jui-lien's collection and because each entry contains no more than the transcription of Yang En-shou's colophon on a particular painting or calligraphy.

The second series of Yen-fu pien is a catalogue of paintings and calligraphy from Tu Jui-lien's and several other collections, none of which was of any significance. Unlike the first series, however, the entries here are of some value because they contain full catalogue information on the paintings: measurements, materials, subject matter, seals, colophons, to whom the paintings belonged, and where they had been previously recorded.

The third series consists of nothing but encomiums on paintings and calligraphy in Tu Jui-lien's collection and is utterly worthless.

92. Lu Hsin-yüan 陸心源, I-ku-t'ang t'i-pa 儀顧堂題跋. 1890. 16 chüan. I-ku-t'ang hsü-pa 儀顧堂續跋, 1892, 16 chüan. (Ferguson, 15, 1). [Library of Congress].

Lu Hsin-yüan (1834-1894) was an avid collector of books and antiquities. I-ku-t'ang t'i-pa is essentially a collection of his study notes on the books in his library, but there are recorded a small number of paintings and calligraphy.

A total of 19 paintings are recorded, seven in chüan 14 and 15 of I-ku-t'ang t'i-pa, and twelve in chüan 15 and 16 of I-ku-t'ang hsü-pa. The entries are lengthy and have information on materials, measurements, inscriptions, colophons and seals. The paintings are catalogued again in Lu Hsin-yüan's Jang-li-kuan kuo-yen lu (q.v.) where they more properly belong.

93. Lu Hsin-yüan 陸心源, Jang-li-kuan kuo-yen lu 穰梨館過眼錄. 1892. 40 chüan. Supplement 16 chüan. (Ferguson, 22, 1). 1892 edition. [Freer].

Lu Hsin-yüan (1834-1894) was a scholar and an avid collector of books and antiquities. His antiquarian interests ranged from bronzes to paintings and calligraphy. Jang-li-kuan kuo-yen lu is a catalogue of 482 paintings and calligraphy, most of which were in his family collection, and the rest belonged to friends.

The items are arranged chronologically regardless of format. The paintings range in date from the Six Dynasties to the Ch'ing, Ming dynasty works being the most numerous. Each entry records the measurements, the inscriptions, colophons and seals. It does not give any information on the subject matter or the technique. Lu Hsin-yüan quotes from older catalogues but does not offer any critical comments of his own. In the cases of those items which did not belong to him, he would give the names of the owners.

The supplement, finished in the same year, catalogues 206 more paintings and calligraphy.

94. Li Yü-fen 李玉棻, Ou-po-lo-shih shu hua kuo-mu k'ao 甌鉢羅室書畫過目考. Preface 1894. 4 chüan, supplement 1 chüan. (Ferguson, 16, 1). MSTS, vol. 25, V/9; ISSCHC facsimile reprint of the 1910 edition (1970).

Li Yü-fen lived in the late Ch'ing dynasty but his exact dates are not known. Ou-po-lo-shih shu hua kuo-mu k'ao is a record of the paintings and calligraphy by 829 Ch'ing dynasty artists he had seen. The scope of the book is limited to the Ch'ing dynasty, beginning with the Four Wangs, Yün Shou-p'ing and Wu Li and ending with Li Yü-fen's contemporaries.

The material is arranged in the following way: nine princes in a section proceding chüan 1; 746 painters and calligraphers in a roughly chronological sequence in chüan 1-4; 17 Buddhist priests, 5 Taoists and 52 women painters and calligraphers in the three chüan of the supplement. For each person, Li Yü-fen provides a brief biography, followed by an enumeration of his or her works he had seen; these are tersely described.

As a catalogue, the information is far from complete. The merit of this compilation lies in the large number of Ch'ing dynasty painters and calligraphers assembled.

95. Shao Sung-nien 邵松年, Ku-yüan ts'ui-lu 古緣萃錄. 1904. 18 chüan. (Ferguson, 5, 2). 1904 edition. [Freer].

Shao Sung-nien lived in the late Ch'ing dynasty, but his exact dates are not known. Ku-yüan ts'ui-lu is a catalogue of his large collection of paintings and calligraphy. A considerable number of pieces were inherited from his uncle Yang Ch'ing-lin 楊慶麟 and they are designated by the name "P'ing-lu-chai 弁廬齋", Yang's studio.

There is no table of contents. Paintings and calligraphy are not put into separate categories and are arranged in a chronological sequence, chüan 1 dealing with T'ang and Sung works, chüan 2 with Yüan, chüan 3-7 with Ming, chüan 7-16 with Ch'ing, and chüan 17-18 with rubbings of calligraphy carved on stone. Each entry contains full information on materials, measurements and a detailed description of the painting. Inscriptions, colophons and seals are recorded. Shao

Sung-nien does not have critical comments for every painting, but when they do occur, they are sharp and astute.

96. Li Pao-hsün 李葆恂, <u>Wu-i-yu-i-chai lun-hua shih</u> 無益有益齋論畫詩. 1909. 2 <u>chüan</u>. (Ferguson, 12, 3). 1909 edition. [Freer].

Li Pao-hsün (1859-1915) was a scholar and connoisseur. He was closely associated with the famous collector Tuan-fang 端方 (1861-1911), advising him on his collection and helping to write some of his catalogues. <u>Wu-i-yu-i-chai lun-hua shih</u> is a record of 99 of the best paintings Li had seen, many of which were in Tuan-fang's collection and are so designated.

The paintings range from the <u>Lo-shen t'u</u> attributed to Ku K'ai-chih (now in the Freer Gallery) to a few of early Ch'ing date, and the majority bear Sung and Yüan attributions. Each entry consists of a verse in four lines with seven characters to each line, followed by a short paragraph in prose. The verse is in appreciation of the painting and is not informative. The notes following give a description of the painting, and occasionally mention some colophons and seals, by no means exhaustively. Dimensions are omitted.

It is regrettable that the information is not as full as it could have been. (A much more complete catalogue, presumably of many of the same paintings, was compiled by Li Pao-hsün in 1899, but the manuscript was destroyed during the Boxer uprising in 1900 and a much mutilated version survives in <u>Hai-wang-ts'un so-chien</u>

shu hua lu, q.v.). Because Wu-i-yu-i-chai lun-hua shih is of such recent date and many of the paintings are still extant, the identification of entries with extant paintings is a matter of certainty.

97. Li Yü-fen 李玉棻, Wang Feng-ch'ang shu hua t'i-pa 王奉常書畫題跋, sometimes referred to as Yen-k'o t'i-pa 煙客題跋. 1909. 2 chüan. (Ferguson, 4, 8). 1909 edition. [Freer].

Li Yü-fen (q.v.) lived in the late Ch'ing dynasty and he was much concerned with Ch'ing painting. Wang Feng-ch'ang shu hua t'i-pa is a collection of 175 inscriptions and colophons by the early Ch'ing master, Wang Shih-min 王時敏 (1592-1680). Of these, 44 are inscriptions on his own paintings, and 131 are colophons on paintings and calligraphy by others. In his preface, Li Yü-fen states that these were copied from his manuscript copy borrowed from a descendant of Sung Lo 宋犖 (1634-1713).

The 175 items are arranged in an arbitrary order. Comparison of two particular inscriptions in the text (chüan 2:10a and chüan 2:13a-14a) with their extant originals (Wang Shih-min's inscription on his Six Album Leaves in the Styles of Old Masters [Freer Gallery, acc. no. 62.29] and his colophon on Wang Hui's Dwelling in the Fu-ch'un Mountains after Hang Kung-wang [Freer Gallery, acc. no. 50.19]) reveals minor differences. The explanation for these is that Wang Shih-min probably kept copies of his inscriptions and colophons and went on polishing them as literary compositions.

Not having any other information, this text does not help in any way in the identification of the paintings on which the inscriptions and colophons were written. But it does present a sizable body of Wang Shih-min's thoughts on paintings, provided one can wade through his rather ponderous literary style.

98. P'ang Yüan-chi 龐元濟, Hsü-chai ming-hua lu 虛齋名畫錄. 1909. 16 chüan. Supplement in 4 chüan, 1924; addendum, 1925. (Ferguson, 12, 9). ISSCHC facsimile reprint of the original editions (1972).

P'ang Yüan-chi (ca. 1865-1949) was a distinguished Shanghai collector. Hsü-chai ming-hua lu is a catalogue of his collection of paintings which was among the most important of his time.

The paintings are divided according to format and arranged chronologically. Chüan 1-6 are devoted to 124 handscrolls, chüan 7-10 to 345 hanging scrolls, and chüan 11-16 to 88 albums. The earliest paintings have T'ang attributions and the latest are Ch'ing in date. Each entry gives dimensions, materials and a very terse description of the painting. Inscriptions, colophons and seals are meticulously and exhaustively transcribed. In these respects, the catalogue is a model of clarity, consistency and thoroughness. But there are no critical comments by P'ang Yüan-chi on the paintings, nor is there any information on where they were previously recorded.

Because the collection was formed relatively recently

and stayed intact well into the 20th century, a considerable number of the paintings went into Western collections. These can be definitely identified with certain paintings recorded in Hsü-chai ming-hua lu, thanks to the full documentation of their seals and colophons.

A supplement in 4 chüan entitled Hsü-chai ming-hua hsü-lu was compiled and printed in 1924. It is a catalogue of about 200 paintings acquired by P'ang Yüan-chi between the years 1909 and 1924. The arrangement differs from that of its predecessor in that all the paintings are arranged chronologically regardless of format. The contents of each entry remains much as in the 1909 catalogue, with the exception that the description of the painting is much more detailed. In his preface to hsü-lu, P'ang Yüan-chi states that in this respect he models himself on An Ch'i's Mo-yüan hui-kuan (q.v.).

Bound with chüan 4 of hsü-lu is an addendum cataloguing six paintings acquired by P'ang Yüan-chi in the spring of 1925.

99. Ts'ai Yü-mou 蔡毓茂, Chu-t'ang wen kao 竹堂文稿. 1 chüan. (Ferguson, 6, 7).

This text has not been located. According to Ferguson, who used a manuscript copy, Ts'ai Yü-mou was a Ch'ing person.

100. Chin-liang 金梁, Sheng-ching ku-kung shu hua lu 盛京故宮書畫錄. Preface dated 1913. 7 tse. (Ferguson, 12, 6). ISTP, vol. 21, no. 172.

Chin-liang was a Manchu scholar who was active in the very last years of the Ch'ing dynasty and continued to be active as a literary editor well into the 1930's. Sheng-ching ku-kung shu hua lu is a catalogue of about 450 paintings and calligraphy in the Ch'ing imperial collection stored in the Hsiang-feng-ko 翔鳳閣 in the Summer Palace at Sheng-ching (Mukden). The catalogue was begun in 1908 and completed in 1913. The collection stored at the Hsiang-feng-ko was by no means the entire collection at Mukden; there were other halls in the Summer Palace whose holdings were not recorded.

The items are divided into seven categories: handscrolls, hanging scrolls, albums, sutras, panels, horizontal tablets and couplets. In each category, the Ch'ien-lung emperor's creations head the list, followed by other people's calligraphy and paintings arranged in a chronological sequence. Each entry gives the dimensions, notes the materials, and records the seals and colophons. Occasionally Chin-liang contributes some critical comments

The Hsiang-feng-ko holdings were later moved to the Ku-wu ch'en-lieh-so 古物陳列所 in Peking (see Nei-wu-pu ku-wu ch'en-lieh-so shu hua mu-lu, q.v.), and a small number of the paintings are now in the National Central Museum in Taiwan and recorded in Ku-kung shu hua lu (q.v.).

101. Ch'en K'uei-lin 陳夔麟, Pao-yü-ko shu hua lu 寶迂閣書畫錄. 1915. 4 chüan. (Ferguson, 19, 1). [Stanford University Art Library].

Ch'en K'uei-lin (born ca. 1855) had a collection of several hundred paintings and calligraphy. <u>Pao-yü-ko shu hua lu</u> is a catalogue of a selection of the better examples in the collection: 50 handscrolls, 107 hanging scrolls and 63 albums. About 75% is paintings, which are arranged with the calligraphy in a chronological order regardless of format. There are several paintings which bear Five Dynasties, Sung and Yüan attributions, but the vast majority are Ming and Ch'ing.

The entries give information on materials and describe the paintings; dimensions are not given. Inscriptions and colophons are transcribed and seals are recorded. There are references to and lengthy quotations from earlier texts where some of the paintings are recorded. Ch'en K'uei-lin ends every entry with a paragraph of his critical comments and results of his research. This is a good catalogue and some of the paintings are extant.

102. Li Pao-hsün 李葆恂, <u>Hai-wang-ts'un so-chien shu hua lu ts'an-kao</u> 海王村所見書畫錄殘稿. 1916. 1 <u>chüan</u>. (Ferguson, 10, 6). 1916 edition. [Freer].

The preface dated 1914 by Li Fang 李放, the son of Li Pao-hsün (1859-1915) (<u>q.v.</u>), states that <u>Hai-wang-ts'un so-chien shu hua lu</u> was completed by his father in 1899. It was in 10 <u>chüan</u>. The manuscript was destroyed during the Boxer uprising in the following year, and the present text was resurrected from an incomplete first draft; hence the "ts'an-kao" of the title.

Hai-wang-ts'un, sometimes referred to as Liu-li-ch'ang 琉璃廠, was and still is the area of antique shops in Peking. In this much reduced text are recorded 14 paintings and two pieces of calligraphy which Li Pao-hsün saw there. A number of these are also recorded in Li Pao-hsün's other compilation, Wu-i-yu-i-chai lun-hua shih (q.v.).

In each entry, Li records measurements and materials; he notes the important seals and transcribes the colophons. At the end of the entry is a paragraph of his comments. This is an interesting catalogue, particularly as some of the paintings are extant, and the loss of the greater part of the original text is regrettable.

103. Ch'ung I 崇彝, Hsüan-hsüeh-chai shu hua yü-mu pi-chi 選學齋書畫寓目筆記. 1921. 3 chüan. (Ferguson, 16, 3). 1921 edition in GMS, no. 92. [Freer microfilm].

Ch'ung I was a modern collector and connoisseur active in the first decades of the 20th century. Hsüan-hsüeh-chai shu hua yü-mu pi-chi is a catalogue of the paintings and calligraphy he saw between the years 1906 and 1921.

The items catalogued are arranged according to format. Chüan 1 records 22 paintings in the form of handscrolls ranging from the Sung to the Ch'ing dynasty, and 12 pieces of calligraphy. Chüan 2 records 15 albums

of paintings of late Ming and early Ch'ing date, and
ten albums of calligraphy. Chüan 3 records 31 paintings in the form of hanging scrolls ranging from Sung
to Ch'ing, and nine pieces of calligraphy.

The catalogue is exemplary. Materials, dimensions,
description, inscriptions, colophons, seals, references
to discussions in earlier catalogues, critical comments,
and current owner— all the information that a reader
could wish for is there. Apart from its excellence,
the catalogue is valuable because some of the paintings
are extant, as is to be expected of objects seen so
recently.

A supplement in 3 chüan records 23 handscrolls,
15 albums and 31 hanging scrolls as well as some calligraphy. It was published in 1941 and the items were
seen by Ch'ung I in the previous 20 years. It is also
in Gunnar Martins Samling av Kinesisk och Japansk
Litteratur, no. 92.

104. Wang Shih-yüan 汪士元, Lu-yün-lou shu hua chi
麓雲樓書畫記. 1922. 1 chüan. (Ferguson,
19, 6). [Stanford University Art Library].

Wang Shih-yüan was a modern collector. Lu-yün-lou
shu hua chi is a catalogue of his collection of about
130 paintings, arranged in a chronological order with a
few pieces of calligraphy. Several of the paintings
bear Sung and Yüan attributions, but the majority of them
are Ming and Ch'ing.

The entries are brief. They give approximate dimensions, information on materials and terse descriptions of the paintings. They note colophons but do not transcribe them. There are no critical comments. Among the paintings are some interesting items which must still be extant.

105. Ho Yü 何煜 and others, Nei-wu-pu ku-wu ch'en-lieh-so shu hua mu-lu 內務部古物陳列所書畫目錄. 1925. 14 chüan, supplement 3 chüan, addendum 2 chüan. (Ferguson, 4, 1). 1925 edition. [Freer].

This is a catalogue of those paintings and calligraphy in the Ch'ing imperial collection which were stored in the two summer palaces at Feng-t'ien 奉天 (Mukden) and Jehol 熱河 in Manchuria. In 1913, the second year after the establishment of the Republic, these items were moved to and exhibited at the Wen-hua-tien 文華殿 and the Wu-ying-tien 武英殿 in Peking, and they came under the custodianship of the Nei-wu-pu ku-wu ch'en-lieh-so 內務部古物陳列所 (The Bureau of Exhibition of Antiquities, Ministry of the Interior).

Chüan 1-4 are devoted to calligraphy. The paintings, catalogued in chüan 5-14, are arranged chronologically under the following categories: albums (428), handscrolls (214), hanging scrolls (727), screen panels (323), horizontal hanging scrolls (50), diptychs (12), album of painting and calligraphy combined (1), handscrolls of painting and calligraphy combined (18), hanging scrolls of painting and calligraphy combined

(4), screen panels of painting and calligraphy combined (41), portraits (15 albums), hanging scrolls of portraits (83), fan paintings and calligraphy combined (1301). The supplement deals with k'o-ssu and the addendum deals with sutras.

Each entry gives the measurements of the painting and a terse description of the subject matter; it also records the seals and colophons. There are no comments by the compilers. For the more important paintings, there are quotations of discussions in earlier catalogues.

A comparison with Sheng-ching ku-kung shu hua lu (q.v.) shows the entries in that catalogue to be more detailed than those in the present one. It also shows that a number of items recorded there are not in the present catalogue, indicating that they had been lost between the years 1913 and 1925.

In the 1930's, the antiquities here catalogued were evacuated from Peking along with the antiquities of the Palace Museum by the personnel of that institution. After World War II, the Bureau of Exhibition of Antiquities was abolished, and the objects came under the custodianship of the Central Museum. In the winter of 1948, the most important pieces from the collection were moved to Taiwan along with the objects of the Palace Museum. The paintings and calligraphy in the two museums were catalogued in Ku-kung shu hua lu (q.v.), and those in the Central Museum are designated "Chung po 中博". Pieces so designated number 231 paintings and 59 pieces of calligraphy in both the Cheng-mu and Chien-mu sections. These figures are drastically smaller than those in

Nei-wu-pu ku-wu ch'en-lieh-so shu hua mu-lu, thus indicating that the bulk of that collection was left in Nanking and is probably still there.

106. Kuo Pao-ch'ang 郭葆昌, <u>Chih-chai shu hua lu</u> 觶齋書畫錄. 1926. 1 <u>chüan</u>. (Ferguson, 19, 5). ISSCHC facsimile reprint of the 1926 edition (1970).

Kuo Pao-ch'ang is best known in the West as the supervisor of the manufacture of the official Hung-hsien 洪憲 ceramic ware at Ching-te Chen 景德鎮 during the administration of Yüan Shih-k'ai 袁世凱 (1913-16), and as the author of the introduction to the catalogue of the International Exhibition of Chinese Art held in London in 1934-35. He was equally knowledgeable on painting, and served as a special consultant to the Palace Museum in Peiping on his two specialities from 1928 to 1931.

<u>Chih-chai shu hua lu</u> is a catalogue of 47 paintings and 19 pieces of calligraphy in his collection, arranged together in chronological sequence. Each entry gives the dimensions and a brief description of the painting. It records the seals, and notes the colophons but does not transcribe them. Kuo does not offer any critical comments, but occasionally he quotes from earlier catalogues where the paintings are recorded and discussed. Kuo Pao-ch'ang was a discriminating collector, and some of the paintings are extant and in Western collections.

107. Kuan Mien-chün 關冕鈞, San-ch'iu-ko shu hua lu 三秋閣書畫錄. 1928. 2 chüan. (Ferguson, 3, 1). 1928 edition. [University of Chicago Library].

Kuan Mien-chün was a modern collector. San-ch'iu-ko shu hua lu is a catalogue of 135 paintings and 50 pieces of calligraphy selected from his collection.

The paintings and calligraphy are arranged together in a chronological sequence. Each entry gives the dimensions of the painting and records the seals and colophons. There is no description of the painting except in the case of album leaves. Occasionally, Kuan Mien-chün contributes a few comments on the people who had written colophons and/or affixed seals to the paintings. Otherwise, there are no critical comments. At the end of the catalogue is a list of the couplets and fan paintings and calligraphy in the collection.

108. Ch'in Ch'ien 秦潛, P'u hua chi yü 曝畫紀餘. 1929. 12 chüan. (Ferguson, 19, 4). 1929 edition. [Freer].

P'u hua chi yü is a catalogue of 339 paintings in the collection of the compiler's grandfather Ch'in Ping-wen 秦炳文 (1803-1873) as well as 399 paintings by him.

Chüan 1, 3, 5, 7, 9 and 11 are devoted to handscrolls, albums, hanging scrolls, horizontal hanging scrolls, fan paintings and miscellaneous respectively. The vast majority of these are of Ming and Ch'ing date. Chüan 2, 4, 6, 8, 10 and 12 are devoted to paintings in corresponding format by Ch'in Ping-wen.

The entries record seals, inscriptions and colophons. Some of the measurements given are not exact. Comments by the compiler are few and far between.

S.1. Chu Ching-hsüan 朱景玄, T'ang-ch'ao ming-hua lu 唐朝名畫錄. 1 chüan. MSTS, vol. 8, II/6; ISTP, vol. 8, no. 59.

Chu Ching-hsüan was active in the second quarter of the ninth century, but his exact dates are not known. T'ang-ch'ao ming-hua lu deals with 97 artists of the T'ang dynasty, and on internal evidence, Soper suggests that the work be assigned to the early 840's.

With the exception of three imperial princes and three painters put into the i-p'in (untrammelled) category, the painters are graded qualitatively into three divisions of "inspired", "excellent" and "competent", and within each of these, into three subdivisions of top, middle and bottom.

The work consists of a preface, a table of contents in which the name of each artist is supplemented with a list of his special themes, and the text where each of the 97 artists has an entry to himself in which his biography is given, anecdotes relating to him recounted, and some of his paintings discussed. Most relevant to our purpose is that in these discussions, specific titles are often mentioned, and some of the paintings are tersely described.

For a translation of this text into English, see Alexander C. Soper, "T'ang Ch'ao Ming Hua Lu", in Artibus Asiae, vol. 21 (1958), pp. 204-230.

S.2. Chang Yen-yüan 張彥遠, Li-tai ming-hua chi 歷代名畫記. 847 A.D. 10 chüan. ISTP, vol. 8, no. 58. Punctuated edition: in Chung-kuo mei-shu lun-chu ts'ung-k'an 中國美術論著叢刊 (Peking, 1963). [Freer]. Punctuated and annotated edition (Shanghai, 1964).

Chang Yen-yüan's exact dates are not known. Li-tai ming-hua chi was completed in 847 A.D. and he was still active in 874 A.D.

The book can be divided into two parts. The first part, chüan 1-3, consists of discussions of various topics of painting: (1) the origins of painting; (2) the vicissitudes of great collections of painting; (3) a list of 370 painters from the earliest times to the T'ang dynasty; (4) Hsieh Ho's "Six Canons"; (5) landscapes, rocks and trees; (6) the transmission of the art of the painting in the Six Dynasties period; (7) the brush method of Ku K'ai-chih, Lu T'an-wei, Chang Seng-yu and Wu Tao-tzu; (8) styles of painting, supplies, and the making of copies and tracings; (9) prices and quality; (10) connoisseurship, collecting and appreciation; (11) some examples of colophons; (12) some examples of seals; (13) mounting, backing, borders and rollers; (14) frescoes in Buddhist and Taoist temples in Ch'ang-an and Lo-yang; appended to this section is a list of the frescoes which survived the destruction of Buddhist temples in 845 A.D.; and (15) a list of 97 treasured paintings through the ages.

For our purpose, (14) and (15) are the most interesting sections from this part of the book as they contain specific titles of paintings.

Part two of the book, chüan 4-10, deals with the 370 painters in section (3) above, ranging from the period of the legendary emperors to the T'ang dynasty. As in Chu Ching-hsüan's T'ang-ch'ao ming-hua lu (q.v.), each artist has an entry to himself, with brief biographical details, anecdotes about him, and discussions of his paintings. In these discussions, beginning with the Chin 晉 dynasty, many specific titles are mentioned, usually of paintings which Chang Yen-yüan had actually seen. This part of the book is important for our purpose, for it is an early record of the titles of some of the paintings by Six Dynasties and T'ang artists.

For an introduction to Li-tai ming-hua chi and a translation of chüan 1-3 into English, see William R.B. Acker, Some T'ang and Pre-T'ang Texts on Chinese Painting (Leiden, 1954), pp. XLVII-L and 59-382.

S.3. Huang Hsiu-fu 黃休復, I-chou ming-hua lu 益州名畫錄, sometimes referred to as Ch'eng-tu ming-hua lu 成都名畫錄. Preface dated 1006. 3 chüan. WSSHY, chüan 9. [Freer].

Huang Hsiu-fu, whose exact dates are not known, was a Northern Sung scholar and connoisseur who was active in the late 10th-early 11th century. I-chou ming-hua lu deals with 58 artists from the mid-8th century to the mid-10th century who were active in I-chou, the present-day Szechuan province. It has a preface by Huang Hsiu-fu's friend Li T'ien 李畋, dated 1006.

During the first half of the 10th century, I-chou was under the state of Shu which, with its centre at Ch'eng-tu, was one of the two relatively peaceful regions in China in the upheaval of the Five Dynasties period, and a number of artists from Ch'ang-an and elsewhere had taken refuge there. The other centre was Nanking, capital of the Nan T'ang. In both these places painting flourished. From what little we know about the Shu school, it seems to have been the more avant-garde of the two. One feature of the school was the development of ink painting of the so-called i-p'in (untrammelled) style.

Huang Hsiu-fu's approach resembles that of Chu Ching-hsüan in T'ang-ch'ao ming-hua lu (q.v.) and the artists are graded into four categories. Where Huang differs from Chu is in (a) his definition of the "untrammelled" category which he places qualitatively above the three categories of "inspired", "excellent" and "competent", and in (b) not subdividing the "inspired" category into top, middle and bottom. Each of the 58 artists has an entry to himself, with very brief biographical information and fairly lengthy discussions of his paintings. Specific titles are sometimes mentioned, and in the cases of artists who painted frescoes, the names of the temples where their works were executed are given.

This text is valuable for its information on the artists of an important centre of painting in the Five Dynasties period and the 150 years previous to that.

S.4. Liu Tao-ch'un 劉道醇, Wu-tai ming-hua pu-i
五代名畫補遺. Preface dated 1060.
1 chüan. ISSCHC facsimile reprint of a Ming
edition in the National Central Library (1972).

Liu Tao-ch'un's dates are not known, but he must have lived in the middle decades of the 11th century. According to Ch'en Hsün-chih's 陳洵直 preface dated 1060, the work was compiled to supplement Hu Ch'iao's 胡嶠 Liang-ch'ao ming-hua mu 梁朝名畫目; hence the "pu-i" of the title. Hu's book, which is no longer extant, discussed 43 painters of the Liang dynasty, the first of the five royal houses of the Five Dynasties period, and Liu Tao-ch'un in Wu-tai ming-hua pu-i discusses 21 painters and four sculptors active at Nanking in the remaining four decades of the Five Dynasties period, roughly from 923 to 960 A.D.

The artists are classified into groups according to their specialities: figure painting; landscape; animals, birds and flowers; architecture; and sculpture. Within each group, the painters are graded into the categories of "inspired", "excellent" and "competent". Each artist has an entry with brief biographical information, followed by a discussion of his work; specific titles are rarely mentioned. The inclusion of information on sculptors is a most unusual feature.

S.5. Li Chih 李廌, Te-yü-chai hua-p'in 德隅齋畫品, sometimes abbreviated to Hua-p'in.
1 chüan. MSTS, vol. 18, IV/5; ISTP, vol. 10, no. 69.

Li Chih lived towards the end of the Northern Sung dynasty but his exact dates are not known. A close friend of Su Shih 蘇軾 (1036-1101), Li survived Su by some years. <u>Te-yü-chai hua-p'in</u> is a desscriptive catalogue of part of the painting collection of his patron Chao Ling-chih 趙令畤, a scion of the Sung imperial family. Chao served at Hsiang-yang 襄陽 in Hupei province in 1098 and left the bulk of his collection at the capital at K'ai-feng. Li Chih's catalogue deals with the paintings Chao took with him to Hsiang-yang.

The 25 works, by famous masters ranging from the late T'ang through to the 11th century, include examples of secular figure painting, Buddhist painting. mythological painting, landscape, birds and flowers, animals, and architectural painting. Each entry consists of a description and a discussion of the painting, and a few seals are mentioned. The catalogue is of unusual interest as it is rare to have actual descriptions of paintings in early extant texts.

For an introduction to <u>Te-yü-chai hua-p'in</u> and a translation into English, see Alexander C. Soper, "A Northern Sung Descriptive Catalogue of Paintings", in <u>Journal of the American Oriental Society</u>, vol. 69 (1949), pp. 18-33.

S.6. Wang Yün 王惲, <u>Shu hua mu-lu</u> 書畫目錄.
Preface dated 1276. 1 <u>chüan</u>. MSTS, vol. 18, IV/6; ISTP, vol. 17, no. 154.

Wang Yün (1227-1304) was a scholar and a high-ranking official in the early years of the Yüan dynasty. In his preface to Shu hua mu-lu, dated 1276, he recounts how he came to see the 147 pieces of calligraphy and 81 paintings in the Yüan imperial collection here recorded.

With a few exceptions, the paintings are recorded by title only, which is most regrettable. (One of the exceptions is the Portraits of Fourteen Emperors attributed to Yen Li-pen; the entry has enough information for the painting to be identified with reasonable certainty as the Portraits of Thirteen Emperors now in the Museum of Fine Arts, Boston.) The brevity of the entries notwithstanding, Shu hua mu-lu is of great interest, firstly because of its early date, and secondly because of the intrinsic interest in the fact that it is a record of the Yüan imperial collection. It should dispel to a certain extent the supposition that the Yüan represented a dark age in the history of imperial collections. It is generally thought that the Northern Sung collection was lost at the sack of K'ai-feng, that the replacement so painstakingly built up by the Southern Sung emperors met a similar fate at the end of the dynasty, and that there was no imperial collection to speak of until the Ming.

A comparison of the titles in Shu hua mu-lu with those in Sung Chung-hsing-kuan-ko ch'u-ts'ang t'u-hua chi (q.v.) suggests that nineteen of the 81 paintings recorded in the former were in the Southern Sung imperial collection. These constituted a link, however tenuous, between the two collections.

S.7. Yüeh-sheng so-ts'ang shu hua pieh-lu 悅生所藏書畫別錄 . 1 chüan. MSTS, vol. 20, IV/10; ISTP, vol. 17, no. 151.

Yüeh-sheng so-ts'ang shu hua pieh-lu is a list of some of the paintings in the collection of Chia Ssu-tao 賈似道 (died 1275), the infamous prime minister in the reign of Sung Li-tsung (reigned 1225-1264), whose favourite consort was Chia Ssu-tao's sister. Because of his position and power, Chia was able to amass an enormous collection, and some of his paintings are said to have been given to him from the imperial collection.

This list, consisting of 58 paintings and 42 pieces of calligraphy, is culled from Yüeh-sheng pieh-lu 悅生別錄 . The items are listed by title only and there is no other information.

S.8. T'ang Hou 湯垕 , Hua chien 畫鑑 . 1 chüan. MSTS, vol. 11, III/2; ISTP, vol. 11, no. 82. Edition punctuated and rendered into modern Chinese: in Chung-kuo hua-lun ts'ung-shu 中國畫論叢書 (Peking, 1962). [Freer].

T'ang Hou is labelled a Sung man in some Chinese texts, but although his exact dates are not known, it appears that his life span fell entirely within the Yüan dynasty. By internal evidence Hua chien can be dated to the 1320's.

The work is a survey of painting traced through the principal practitioners from the Three Kingdoms period to the Sung and Chin 金 . In the cases of some painters, there are general critical comments as well as descriptions and discussions of specific paintings, while in the cases of others, statements are very brief. The arrangement of the book is good.

S.9. Hsia Wen-yen 夏文彥, T'u-hui pao chien 圖繪寶鑑. Preface dated 1365. 5 chüan. ISTP, vol. 11, no. 83.

Hsia Wen-yen was a 14th century collector and his preface to T'u-hui pao chien is dated 1365.

Chüan 1 is devoted to discussions of the theory of painting and miscellaneous topics. The rest of the book consists of entries on some 1,500 painters ranging from the Three Kingdoms period to the Yüan, including some non-Chinese painters. Each entry has brief biographical information on the artist and a discussion in general terms of his paintings. Specific titles are very seldom mentioned.

Because of the great number of biographies it had gathered together, the book was much quoted by Ming and especially Ch'ing writers, and it became a standard reference. But a closer examination suggests that it does not deserve the high regard it enjoyed for so long. Its material is drawn from Li-tai ming-hua chi, T'u-hua chien-wen chih, Hsüan-ho hua p'u (qq.v.) and other early texts and catalogues. Hsia Wen-yen took sections from his various sources without paying attention to their individual arrangement and without devising an arrangement of his own. The result is that other than the broad grouping of artists by dynasty, there is virtually no organization.

As it appears in ISTP, T'u-hui pao chien has a sixth chüan compiled by Han Ang 韓昂 in 1519 consisting of biographies of 114 Ming artists. It also incorporates a supplement for some of the omissions in Hsia Wen-yen's text.

S.10. Wang Chih-teng 王穉登, Wu-chün tan-ch'ing chih 吳郡丹青志. Preface dated 1563. 1 chüan. MSTS, vol. 6, II/2; ISTP, vol. 12, no. 95.

Wang Chih-teng (1535-1612) was a native of Suchou and a noted connoisseur. In Wu-chün tan-ch'ing chih he discusses 25 Suchou painters ranging from the 14th century to his own time, and puts them into seven categories.

Any reader whose hopes have been raised by Sirén's grandiose translated title, The Chronicle of Suchou Painters, will be bitterly disappointed. The work is short, its scope ill-defined, the choice of painters for inclusion as well as the grading arbitrary. The discussions of different painters are too general; they are not informative on biographical matters, style, or specific paintings. This is the work by a young man written to while away the time when he was confined to bed by illness.

S.11. Wu Ch'i-chen 吳其貞, Shu hua chi 書畫記.
6 chüan. Facsimile reprint of the copy in SKCS (Shanghai, 1962). [Freer].

Wu Ch'i-chen was a connoisseur of painting and calligraphy, active in the decades spanning the end of Ming and the beginning of Ch'ing. He knew all the collectors in Suchou, Hangchou and Yangchou, and Shu hua chi is a record of the 1,256 paintings and specimens of calligraphy which he saw in private collections in those cities in the years between 1635 and 1677. It was completed probably in 1677 or shortly after, but was printed for the first time in 1962.

The items are arranged not chronologically, but in the order in which they were seen by Wu in the forty-two years. This is admittedly not the best arrangement from the point of view of the research worker. Each entry describes the condition of the painting, records the artist's signature and seals, if any, and notes but does not record colophons by previous connoisseurs. Occasionally, measurements are given. Many of the entries are terse, and at first glance the book may appear to be rather erratic and therefore not very useful. In fact, the shortcomings of terseness and inconsistency are to a certain extent compensated for by two excellent features. First, the concluding remarks in nearly every entry consist of such information as the current ownership of the piece, the date Wu saw it, and sometimes the vicissitudes undergone by a painting in the recent past. Thanks to this type of information, the transmission of certain paintings can be more fully reconstructed. (An example of this is the invaluable information furnished by Wu

for the reconstruction of the most crucial part of the
history of Huang Kung-wang's Fu-ch'un shan-chü t'u.)
Second, and perhaps more important, is the remarkable
critical faculty which enabled Wu to cut through the
jungle of impedimenta in the form of signatures, inscriptions, colophons and seals, and to go straight to
the painting itself, often resulting in a terse pro-
nouncement: "Later than attribution". This lack of
gullibility is most refreshing and the more impressive
for being so rare among Chinese connoisseurs. The
catalogue is not free from errors, but these are usually
minor ones, the result of lapses of memory and of inadequate notes being taken at the time the paintings
were seen.

Before 1962, Shu hua chi was little known because
it was never printed and because it fell under the shad-
ow of Ch'ien-lung's censorship. The text was incorporated into Ssu-k'u ch'üan-shu 四庫全書, the "Complete Library in Four Branches of Literature" compiled
from 1773 to 1785, a compilation of all available books
with the exception of those considered to be seditious
to the regime or to be intellectually or morally offen-
sive. What gave offence in Shu hua chi was Wu Ch'i-chen's
description of an erotic painting attributed to Chou Fang
entitled Ch'un-hsiao pi-hsi t'u 春宵秘戲圖. The
book is listed in Ssu-k'u ch'üan-shu tsung-mu t'i-yao
四庫全書總目提要, a review completed in 1781 of
the 3,450 titles to be included in, as well as the 6,780
titles to be excluded from, Ssu-k'u ch'üan-shu. It is
still listed in Ssu-k'u ch'üan-shu chien-ming mu-lu
四庫全書簡明目錄, a simple list compiled in 1782

of the 3,450 titles copied into the library, or more
specifically, in the version printed in Hangchou in
1784, but not in the official version printed in
Canton in 1868. The conclusion to be drawn is that
shortly after 1784, the "pornographic" content of
Shu hua chi came to the notice of the emperor's cen-
sors and the title was suppressed from chien-ming mu-lu.
Fortunately, the book has survived in Ssu-k'u ch'üan-shu
although the entry on Chou Fang's painting no longer
exists. The 1962 edition is a facsimile reprint of the
manuscript copy from one of the four original sets of
Ssu-k'u ch'üan-shu now in the Palace Museum in Peking.

S.12. Ku Fu 顧復, P'ing-sheng chuang-kuan
平生壯觀. Preface dated 1692. 10 chüan.
First edition based on manuscript copy in the
Chekiang Cultural Bureau (Shanghai, 1962).
[Freer]. ISSCHC facsimile reprint of a manu-
script copy (1970).

Ku Fu was a connoisseur of painting and calligraphy active in Nanking and Suchou in the middle and
late 17th century. His exact dates are not known, but
his own preface is dated in correspondence to 1692.
Also dated 1692 is the preface by Hsü Ch'ien-hsüeh
徐乾學 (1631-1694), a close friend of Ku Fu's brother Ku Wei-yüeh 顧維岳. From certain statements
in P'ing-sheng chuang-kuan, it is deduced that Ku Fu
was friendly with Wang Shih-min, Wu Li and Wang Hui.
Also, from certain sentiments expressed towards Ch'ien
Hsüan, Chao Meng-fu and other Southern Sung-Yüan

artists, it is conjectured that Ku Fu was a Ming patriot and remained so under the Ch'ing dynasty.

P'ing-sheng chuang-kuan is a catalogue of the paintings and calligraphy which Ku had seen. Chüan 1-5 are devoted to calligraphy, and chüan 6-10 to paintings which range from the Six Dynasties to works by Tung Ch'i-ch'ang of the late Ming, arranged in a chronological order. The entries are fairly brief; each one as a rule gives a description of the painting and takes note of, but does not record, the colophons. Approximate measurements are sometimes given, not at all consistently. Ku Fu does not pay much attention to seals, nor does he always give references to records of paintings in earlier catalogues. There is usually a paragraph of comments on each of the major painters, and comments on individual paintings are astute. This is an interesting catalogue, and some of the paintings recorded are still extant.

Like Wu Ch'i-chen's Shu hua chi (q.v.), P'ing-sheng chuang-kuan was never printed until 1962. It was even less known than Shu hua chi because it was never collected into any ts'ung-shu and had survived in manuscript form.

S.13. Tse Lang 迮朗 , San-wan liu-ch'ien ch'ing hu-chung hua ch'uan lu 三萬六千頃湖中畫船錄 . Preface 1795. 1 chüan. MSTS, vol. 5, I/10; ISTP, vol. 15, no. 132.

Tse Lang was a painter and seal carver active in the late 18th century (chü-jen 1789). San-wan liu-ch'ien ch'ing hu-chung hua ch'uan lu is a catalogue of about 60 paintings he saw between the years 1782 and 1786, when he maintained a boat on the T'ai Hu 太湖, which covers an area of 36,000 ch'ing; hence the title.

While a few of the paintings are pre-Ming, the majority are Ming and Ch'ing. Dimensions are often but not always given. Otherwise the entries give fairly full information on materials, inscriptions, colophons and seals.

S.14.   Shih-ch'ü pao-chi san-pien mu-lu 石渠寶笈三編目錄. 3 tse. Facsimile reprint of a manuscript copy (1917). [Freer].

Shih-ch'ü pao-chi san-pien (q.v.), the third part of the catalogue of the Ch'ing imperial collection of painting and calligraphy, was compiled in 1816 but was not available to the general public until as recently as 1969. In 1917, the antiquarian Lo Chen-yü 羅振玉 (1865-1940) brought out Shih-ch'ü pao-chi san-pien mu-lu, a list of the titles of the paintings and calligraphy catalogued in san-pien. It is not an index in the strict sense of the word, but an excerpt of the table of contents at the beginning of the text. In his postscript dated 1917, Lo Chen-yü states that the list was taken from a manuscript copy from a Japanese collection. The titles gave a tantalizing glimpse of the contents of san-pien.

For 50 years mu-lu served a purpose until it was superseded by the 1969 reprint of the san-pien in the Palace Museum in Taiwan, with its original table of contents plus a comprehensive index prepared by the Museum staff.

S.15.   P'an Cheng-wei 潘正煒, T'ing-fan-lou shu hua chi 聽颿樓書畫記. Preface dated 1843. 5 chüan. Supplement 2 chüan, 1849. MSTS, vol. 19, IV/7; ISTP, vol. 20, nos. 170, 171.

P'an Cheng-wei (1791-1850), a wealthy Hong merchant, was one of the more prominent Cantonese collectors of the 19th century. In his preface, P'an states that the idea of compiling a catalogue of his collection was first suggested to him by his friend Wu Jung-kuang, and it is not surprising that T'ing-fan-lou shu hua chi is so similar to Wu's catalogue, Hsin-ch'ou hsiao-hsia chi (q.v.), completed two years previously in 1841.

The 255 paintings and calligraphy, ranging from T'ang to Ch'ing, are arranged together in chronological sequence regardless of format. There is a table of contents where the price paid for each item is noted. Each entry gives the dimensions and notes the use of either paper or silk, but does not note the use of colours. It transcribes the inscriptions, colophons and seals, but omits P'an Cheng-wei's own colophons. Consequently, we are left in the dark as to his reaction to the paintings, and are without the benefit of his research, if any.

The supplement, completed six years later, records 120 more works arranged and catalogued in the same way.

S.16. Wu Chih-ying 吳之瑛, <u>Hsiao-wan-liu-t'ang ts'ang hua mu</u> 小萬柳堂藏畫目. 1 <u>tse</u>. 1918. GMS, no. 87. [Freer microfilm].

Wu Chih-ying (died 1933) and her husband Lien Ch'üan 廉泉 (died 1931) were collectors of paintings. In 1918 they found themselves in debt to the amount of 20,000 dollars which they were unable to repay, and had to surrender thirty paintings in their collection to the creditor. <u>Hsiao-wan-liu-t'ang ts'ang-hua mu</u> is a tearful record of these thirty paintings by Wang Chien, Wang Hui, Wang Yüan-ch'i, Yün Shou-p'ing and Wu Li; hence the alternate title, <u>Hsiao-wan-liu-t'ang Wang Yün hua mu</u> 小萬柳堂王惲畫目.

The work is strictly speaking not a catalogue in the sense that we have come to understand by that word by 1918. Each entry records only inscriptions and colophons, and contains no other information. However, it is of interest because some of the paintings are not recorded elsewhere. The book is a lithographic edition with the calligraphy by Wu Chih-ying who was a noted calligrapher.

S.17. P'ei Ching-fu 裴景福, <u>Chuang-t'ao-ko shu hua lu</u> 壯陶閣書畫錄. Preface dated 1924. 22 <u>chüan</u>. ISSCHC facsimile reprint of the 1937 edition (1971).

P'ei Ching-fu (1854-1926) inherited a collection of paintings and calligraphy from his father which was formed in the third quarter of the 19th century, and he expanded it significantly. <u>Chuang-t'ao-ko shu hua lu</u>, completed in 1923 and printed posthumously in 1937, is a catalogue of about 700 items in the collection.

The paintings and calligraphy, of roughly equal numbers, are not put into separate categories. They are arranged chronologically regardless of format. These occupy <u>chüan</u> 1-20; the last two <u>chüan</u> deal with those calligraphy items which are in the form of <u>pei</u> and <u>t'ieh</u>.

The earliest paintings have attributions to the Six Dynasties and the latest are Ch'ing. Each entry gives all the relevant information: materials, dimensions, description of painting, signature and inscription of the artist, seals and colophons, including P'ei's own colophons. There are detailed discussions of records of the paintings in earlier catalogues and how they differ from the documentation on his paintings. The assessment of his paintings after such investigations appears to be sound and fair.

This is an example of the kind of solid catalogue which we have come to expect from serious compilations of such recent date. A number of the items in this catalogue are extant.

S.18. National Palace Museum, <u>Ku-kung i-i shu-chi shu hua mu-lu ssu-chung</u> 故宮已佚書籍書畫目錄四種. Peking, 1934. [Freer].

After the Revolution of 1911, the Hsüan-t'ung emperor was not immediately deposed. On the contrary, he was accorded preferential treatment and allowed to stay in the Forbidden City where he continued to use his reign title and carry on as if the Revolution had not taken place. This anomaly lasted for thirteen years and it was not until November 5, 1924, that P'u-i 溥儀 and his family were forced to leave the palace and to surrender his imperial seals. The former imperial art collection naturally became national property, and a committee consisting of a chairman and fifteen members was set up to deal with all the problems arising from the transfer of ownership.

In 1925, the Committee came upon three lists of paintings, calligraphy and printed books which had been removed from the collection. The longest one, entitled "Items awarded to P'u-chieh 溥傑 [P'u-i's brother]", lists paintings, calligraphy and printed books numbering nearly 1,500 items given to P'u-chieh in a period of five months in 1921. Many of these are choice items. The Committee published the lists in Ku-kung i-i shu-chi shu hua mu-lu san-chung 故宮已佚書籍書畫目錄三種 in 1926. Strictly speaking, there were four, not three, lists, and in 1934, a slightly revised edition was published with the title altered to ssu-chung. Many of the items in the fourth list were actually borrowed and later returned.

A number of the paintings in these lists are now in American and Japanese collections.

S.19. Wan-yen Ching-hsien 完顏景賢, San-yü-t'ang shu hua mu 三虞堂書畫目. 2 chüan. 1933. [Freer].

Wan-yen Ching-hsien was a Manchu connoisseur of the late Ch'ing dynasty and a close friend of the eminent collector Tuan-fang 端方 (1861-1911). He kept a record of the paintings and calligraphy in his own collection and those he had seen. After his death, the manuscript was secured by the artist Su Tsung-jen 蘇宗仁, who edited it and arranged to have it printed in 1933 with a preface by him.

Seventy-five paintings, ranging from the Six Dynasties to the Ming, are recorded in chüan 2. Most of the entries consist of the titles and very brief notations on their materials and whereabouts. There is no information on dimensions; inscriptions and colophons are not transcribed and very rarely mentioned. The incompleteness of the catalogue is regrettable. A good number of the paintings are extant and some are in Western collections.

S.20. Ch'en Jen-t'ao 陳仁濤, Chin-kuei ts'ang-hua p'ing-shih 金匱藏畫評釋. 2 tse. Hong Kong, 1956. [Freer].

Ch'en Jen-t'ao (1906-1968) was one of the prominent collectors of the 20th century. Chin-kuei ts'ang-hua p'ing-shih is a catalogue of 117 paintings in his collection; a supplement records eight additional paintings. Ranging from the Five Dynasties period to the Ch'ing, the paintings appear to be of good quality, and although some of the oldest ones may not really be as old as their attributions, they are nonetheless fairly early copies preserving the styles and compositions of lost masterpieces.

Each entry gives the materials and measurements of the painting, records the signature, inscriptions, and all the colophons and seals. The work would be a good and useful catalogue if it contained no more information than this. But as the "p'ing-shih" in the title implies, the compilation sets out to be more than a mere catalogue. In addition to the factual information on the painting, Ch'en Jen-t'ao provides the following on each item: (1) a section of comments on the subject matter and style of the painting, running to considerable length in the cases of the more important paintings; (2) a brief biography of the painter; and (3) quotations from earlier catalogues where the painting had been recorded or discussed.

Chin-kuei ts'ang-hua p'ing-shih is an exemplary catalogue in the thoroughness and quality of its research and in the clarity with which its material is organized and presented.

S.21. Ch'en Jen-t'ao 陳仁濤, Ku-kung i-i shu hua mu chiao-chu 故宮已佚書畫目校註. Hong Kong, 1956. [Freer].

Ch'en Jen-t'ao (1906-1968) was a modern collector. This work is an amplified and annotated list of the paintings lost from the former imperial collection.

It is based primarily on Ku-kung i-i shu-chi shu hua mu-lu ssu-chung (q.v.), and its secondary sources are eighteen other publications from which is derived the information on the present ownership of some of the paintings.

This compilation is useful for verifying some of the paintings lost from the former imperial collection. However, the items enumerated here by no means account for all the lost paintings. With the publication of more and more paintings, it is possible to up-date this work and make it more complete. The absence of an index is regrettable.

S.22. National Palace Museum 國立故宮博物院 and National Central Museum 國立中央博物院, Ku-kung shu hua lu 故宮書畫錄. 8 chüan. Taipei, 1956; revised second edition, 1965. [Freer].

Ku-kung shu hua lu is a catalogue of the calligraphy and paintings in the National Palace Museum and the National Central Museum which came under a joint administration after their move to Taiwan in 1948. The items in this catalogue represent the entire holdings in the Department of Calligraphy and Painting in the two museums except for the rubbings, k'o-ssu, embroidery, and fan paintings.

The majority of the items belong to the National Palace Museum and are from the former Ch'ing imperial collection in Peking (see Shih-ch'ü pao-chi and its two supplements, Nan-hsün-tien tsun-ts'ang t'u-hsiang mu, Ch'a-k'u ts'ang-chu t'u-hsiang mu and Nan-hsün-tien t'u-hsiang k'ao, qq.v.). A small number of the items belong to the National Central Museum and are from the former imperial collection kept in the summer palaces in Mukden and Jehol (see Sheng-ching ku-kung shu hua lu and <u>Nei-wu-pu ku-wu ch'en-lieh-so shu hua mu-lu</u>, <u>qq.v.</u>). These are designated "Chung po 中博 " to distinguish them from the National Palace Museum items.

There are three broad divisions in <u>Kung-kung shu hua lu</u>. They are: (1) The <u>Cheng-mu</u> 正目 (the Principal List), consisting of 1,477 items of calligraphy and painting deemed worthy of being catalogued in detail. These include old (pre-Ming) works considered of undisputed authenticity, those famous old (pre-Ming) works whose attributions may be questionable but nevertheless either have an intrinsic value or have acquired a distinguished pedigree, and works of Ming and Ch'ing date considered of undisputed authenticity and high quality. (2) The <u>Chien-mu</u> 簡目 (the Abbreviated or Secondary List), consisting of 3,093 items of calligraphy and painting which in the opinion of the Selection Committee fail to meet any of the three conditions given above. (3) Seventy-eight portraits of past emperors, consorts and sages formerly stored in the Nan-hsün-tien in Peking.

The <u>Cheng-mu</u> occupies <u>chüan</u> 1-6. The first three <u>chüan</u> are devoted to calligraphy, a total of 228 items arranged chronologically within the categories of handscrolls (88), hanging scrolls (38), and albums (102), one <u>chüan</u> given to each format. The paintings, totalling 1,249 items, are likewise arranged in <u>chüan</u> 4-6: handscrolls (162), hanging scrolls (924), and albums (163). These are the three <u>chüan</u> which most concern us.

Each entry consists of the title; its catalogue number;‡ metric measurements of the painting, its front and back mounting, and its end-papers; extensive quotations from the primary sources (<u>Shih-ch'ü pao-chi</u> and its two supplements, <u>qq.v.</u>) and the secondary sources (<u>Shih-ch'ü sui-pi</u> and <u>Hsi-Ch'ing cha chi</u>, <u>qq.v.</u>); meticulous recording of all the seals; and a paragraph by the editors embodying any information not covered by the earlier catalogues, critical comments on conclusions reached in the earlier catalogues with which they disagree, and the results of their independent research.

<u>Chüan</u> 7 deals with 78 portraits of former emperors and the entries follow the pattern set in the earlier <u>chüan</u>. Its primary source is <u>Nan-hsün-tien t'u-hsiang k'ao</u> (<u>q.v.</u>).

<u>Ch'üan</u> 8 contains the <u>Chien-mu</u>. The 3,093 items consist of 531 pieces of calligraphy (handscrolls, 148; hanging scrolls, 129; albums, 254), and 2,562 paintings (handscrolls, 449; hanging scrolls, 1,591; albums, 522). The items are listed by title, followed by the catalogue number, with no additional information.

The decision to separate the items into a <u>cheng-mu</u> and a <u>chien-mu</u> is regrettable. (It seems to be a regressive step when the third part of <u>Shih-ch'ü pao-chi</u> had already abandoned the grading of items into "superior" and "secondary" categories employed in the first and second parts of that catalogue). Regardless of the quality of the <u>Chien-mu</u> items, it would be preferable to have all the items fully catalogued. In the 1965 revised edition, this flaw is remedied to a certain extent, as a number of the items previously in

the Chien-mu are moved to the Cheng-mu and given
the full treatment. It is to be hoped that eventually all the items in the Chien-mu wil be fully
catalogued. Apart from this one flaw, Ku-kung shu
hua lu is an excellent catalogue and a model of consistency and thoroughness. It is an indispensable
guide to that great collection of Chinese painting.

* * * * *

‡The catalogue number system was devised soon after
the founding of the National Palace Museum in 1924,
at the time of the take-over of the objects in the
various palaces and halls. Each hall is designated by
a character from the Ch'ien-tzu wen (Thousand-Character
Classic). A catalogue number consists of a character
indicating the hall in which the piece was found, followed by a number in Chinese characters indicating a
particular box in the hall, and followed by a number
in Arabic numerals indicating its sequence in that
box.

Index of Names

(The numbers refer to entry numbers.)

Acker, William R.B.		S.2
An Ch'i	安岐	57
An Yüan-chung	安元忠	57
Ayurparibhadra	愛育黎拔力八達	17
Chan Ching-feng	詹景鳳	28
Chang Chao	張照	58a, 59a
Chang Ch'eng-chih	張誠之	34
Chang Ch'ou	張丑	33, 34, 35, 36, 37
Chang I-sheng	張以繩	34
Chang Keng	張庚	64
Chang Mou-shih	張茂實	34
Chang Ta-yung	張大鏞	76
Chang T'ai-chieh	張泰階	41
Chang Tan-chia	張誕嘉	34
Chang T'ing-chi	張廷濟	82
Chang Tzu-ho	張子和	34
Chang Wei-ch'ing	張維慶	34
Chang Yen-yüan	張彥遠	S.2
Chang Yüan-su	張元素	34
Chang Yüeh-chih	張約之	34
Chao Ch'i-mei	趙琦美	30, 31
Chao Ling-chih	趙令時	S.5

Ch'en Chi-ju	陳繼儒	39, 43
Ch'en Chuan	陳撰	62
Ch'en Ch'uo	陳焯	65
Ch'en Fu-liang	陳傅良	13
Ch'en Jen-t'ao	陳仁濤	S.20, S.21
Ch'en K'uei	陳騤	11
Ch'en K'uei-lin	陳夔麟	101
Ch'en Tsung-i	陳宗彝	79
Chia-ch'ing emperor	嘉慶	58c, 59c
Chia Ssu-tao	賈似道	S.7
Chiang Kuang-hsü	蔣光煦	83
Chiao Hung	焦竑	30
Ch'ien-lung emperor	乾隆	58a, 58b, 59a, 59b, 60, 61
Ch'in Ch'ien	秦潛	108
Chin-liang	金梁	100
Ch'in Ping-wen	秦炳文	108
Ch'in Ssu-lin	秦四麟	30
Ch'ing-fou-shan-jen	青浮山人	71
Chou Erh-hsüeh	周二學	56
Chou Mi	周密	15
Chou Shih-lin	周石林	23
Chou Yün-ch'ing	周雲青	Preface
Chu Chih-ch'ih	朱赤	45
Chu Ching-hsüan	朱景玄	S.1

Chu Hsi	朱熹	12
Chu I-tsun	朱彝尊	53
Chu Ts'un-li	朱存理	18, 30
Chüeh-fan Te-hung	覺範德洪	8
Ch'ung I	崇彝	103
Fang Chün-i	方濬頤	87
Fei Nien-tz'u	費念慈	75
Ferguson, John C.		Preface
Gulik, R.H. van		56
Haisan	海山	17
Han Ang	韓昂	S.9
Han Shih-neng	韓世能	32, 33
Han T'ai-hua	韓泰華	84
Ho Liang-chün	何良俊	24
Ho Yü	何煜	105
Hsia Wen-yen	夏文彥	S.9
Hsiang-ko-la-chi	祥哥拉吉	17
Hsiang Yüan-pien	項元汴	44
Hsü Ch'ien-hsüeh	徐乾學	S.12
Hsüan-t'ung emperor, see P'u-i		
Hu Chi-t'ang	胡積堂	78
Hu Ch'iao	胡嶠	S.4
Hu Ching	胡敬	58c, 59c, 72, 73
Hua Hsia	華夏	20

Huang Hsiu-fu	黃休復	S.3
Hui-tsung	徽宗	9
Juan Yüan	阮元	68
Kao Shih-ch'i	高士奇	49, 50
Kao-tsung	高宗	11
Ko Chin-lang	葛金烺	89
Ko Ssu-t'ung	葛嗣浵	89
Ku Cheng-i	顧正誼	45
Ku Fu	顧復	S.12
Ku Kung-hsiung	顧公雄	90
Ku T'ing-lin	顧亭林	45
Ku Wei-yüeh	顧維岳	S.12
Ku Wen-pin	顧文彬	75, 90
Ku Yen-wu	顧炎武	45
Kuan T'ing-fen	管庭芬	83
Kuan Mien-chün	關冕鈞	107
K'ung Ch'ih-t'ing	孔熾庭	85
K'ung Kuang-t'ao	孔廣陶	85
K'ung Kuang-yung	孔廣鏞	85
Kuo Jo-hsü	郭若虛	2
Kuo Pao-ch'ang	郭葆昌	106
Lawton, Thomas		57
Li Chih	李廌	S.5
Li Chih-i	李之儀	6

Li Fang	李放	102
Li Jih-hua	李日華	38
Li O	厲鶚	55
Li Pao-hsün	李葆恂	96, 102
Li Tiao-yüan	李調元	67
Li T'ien	李畋	S.3
Li Tso-hsien	李佐賢	86
Li Tsu-nien	李祖年	54
Li Yü-fen	李玉棻	94, 97
Liang Chang-chü	梁章鉅	81
Lien Ch'üan	廉泉	S.16
Liu Tao-ch'un	劉道醇	3, S.4
Lo Chen-yü	羅振玉	50, S.14
Lu Hsin-yüan	陸心源	92, 93
Lu Shih-hua	陸時化	66
Maeda, Robert J.		10
Mao Chin	毛晉	5, 8, 12, 14
Mao Wei	茅維	32
Mi Fei	米芾	4, 9
National Central Museum		S.22
National Palace Museum		S.18, S.22
P'an Cheng-wei	潘正煒	S.15
P'an Shih-huang	潘世璜	75
P'an Tsun-ch'i	潘遵祁	75

P'ang Yüan-chi	龐元濟	98
P'ei Ching-fu	裴景福	S.17
P'ei Hsiao-yüan	裴孝源	1
Pien Yung-yü	卞永譽	47
P'u-chieh	溥傑	S.18
P'u-i	溥儀	S.18
Sengge Ragi, see Hsiang-ko-la-chi		
Shao Sung-nien	邵松年	95
Shen T'ao	沈濤	84
Shen Te-ch'ien	沈德潛	63
Shih-pai-chai chu-jen	十百齋主人	69
Soper, Alexander Coburn		2, S.1, S.5
Su Shih	蘇軾	6, 15, S.5
Su Sung	蘇頌	5
Su Tsung-jen	蘇宗仁	S.19
Sun Ch'eng-tse	孫承澤	46
Sun Hsing-yen	孫星衍	79
Sun Kung	孫鑛	29
Sung Lo	宋犖	54, 97
Tämur	鐵穆耳	17
T'ang Hou	湯垕	S.8
T'ang Yün-mo	湯允謨	16
T'ao Liang	陶樑	77
Teng Ch'un	鄧椿	10

Ting Fu-pao	丁福保	Preface
Ts'ai Yü-mou	蔡毓茂	99
Tse Lang	迮朗	S.13
Tu Chao-pin	都肇斌	63
Tu Jui-lien	杜瑞聯	88
Tu Mu	都穆	19, 63
Tuan-fang	端方	96, S.19
Tung Ch'i-ch'ang	董其昌	39, 40, 71
Tung T'ing	董庭	39
Tung Yu	董逌	7
Vandier-Nicolas, Nicole		4
Wan-yen Ching-hsien	完顏景賢	S.19
Wang Ai-ching	汪愛荊	44
Wang Chieh	王杰	58b, 59b
Wang Chih-teng	王穉登	S.10
Wang K'o-yü	汪砢玉	44
Wang Shan	王掞	54
Wang Shih-chen	王世貞	25, 26, 29
Wang Shih-min	王時敏	97
Wang Shih-mou	王世懋	27
Wang Shih-yüan	汪士元	104
Wang To	王鐸	45
Wang Tse	王澤	78
Wang Wen-chih	王文治	70, 71

Wang Yüan-ch'i	王原祁	51
Wang Yün	王惲	S.6
Wen Chia	文嘉	21
Wu Ch'i-chen	吳其貞	S.11
Wu Chih-ying	吳芝瑛	S.16
Wu Hsi-ch'i	吳錫祺	50
Wu Hsiu	吳修	74
Wu Jung-kuang	吳榮光	80
Wu Pi-chiang	吳辟疆	11
Wu Sheng	吳升	54
Yang Ch'ing-lin	楊慶麟	95
Yang En-shou	楊恩壽	91
Yang Wang-hsiu	楊王休	11
Yang Wu-pu	楊無補	40
Yao Chi-heng	姚際恆	52
Yeh Shih	葉適	14
Yen Sung	嚴嵩	21, 22, 23
Yü Feng-ch'ing	郁逢慶	42
Yü Shao-sung	余紹宋	Preface
Yüan Chüeh	袁桷	17
Yün Shou-p'ing	惲壽平	48

Index of Titles

(The numbers refer to entry numbers.)

Ai-jih-yin-lou shu hua lu 愛日吟樓書畫錄 89
Ch'a-k'u ts'ang-chu t'u-hsiang mu
　　茶庫藏貯圖像目 61
Chen-chi jih lu 真蹟日錄 37
Chen-kuan kung ssu hua shih 貞觀公私畫史 1
Ch'eng-tu ming-hua lu 成都名畫錄, see
　　I-chou ming-hua lu
Chiang-ts'un hsiao-hsia lu 江邨銷夏錄 49
Chiang-ts'un shu hua mu 江村書畫目 50
Ch'ien-shan-t'ang shu hua chi 鈐山堂書畫記 21
Chih-chai shu hua lu 䪥齋書畫錄 106
Chih-chai t'i-pa 止齋題跋 13
Chin-kuei ts'ang-hua p'ing-shih 金匱藏畫評釋 S.20
Chinese Pictorial Art as Viewed by the Connoisseur 56
Ch'ing-ho shu hua fang 清河書畫舫 36
Ch'ing-ho shu hua piao 清河書畫表 34
Ch'ing-hsia-kuan lun-hua chüeh-chü
　　青霞館論畫絕句 74
Ch'ing-i-ko t'i-pa 清儀閣題跋 82
Ch'ing-jung-chu-shih chi 清容居士集 17
The Chronicle of Suchou Painters, see
　　Wu-chün tan-ch'ing chih

Chu-chia ts'ang-hua pu	諸家藏畫簿	67
Chu-t'ang wen-kao	竹堂文稿	99
Chu Wo-an ts'ang shu hua mu	朱卧菴藏書畫目	45
Chuang-t'ao-ko shu hua lu	壯陶閣書畫錄	S.17
Fa-shu ming-hua chien wen piao	法書名畫見聞表	
see Shu hua chien wen piao		
Hai-wang-ts'un so-chien shu hua lu ts'an-kao 海王村所見書畫錄殘稿		102
Hao-ku-t'ang shu hua chi	好古堂書畫記	52
Hsi-Ch'ing cha chi	西清劄記	72
Hsiang-kuan-chai yü-shang pien	湘管齋寓賞編	65
Hsiao-wan-liu-t'ang ts'ang hua mu 小萬柳堂藏畫目		S.16
Hsin-ch'ou hsiao-hsia chi	辛丑銷夏記	80
Hsü-chai ming-hua lu	虛齋名畫錄	98
Hsü-ching-chai yün-yen kuo-yen lu 須靜齋雲烟過眼錄		75
Hsüan-ho hua p'u	宣和畫譜	9
Hsüan-hsüeh-chai shu hua yü-mu pi-chi 選學齋書畫寓目筆記		103
Hua-chan-shih sui-pi	畫禪室隨筆	40
Hua chi	畫繼	10, 44
Hua chien	畫鑑	S.8
Hua chü	畫據	44

Hua fa 畫法		44
Hua p'in 畫品, see Te-yü-chai hua-p'in		
Hua shih 畫史		4
"Hua shih Chen-shang-chai fu chu 華氏真賞齋賦注"		20
Hua-yüan pi-chi 畫苑秘笈		11
Hui-an t'i-pa 晦庵題跋		12
Hung-tou-shu-kuan shu hua chi 紅豆樹館書畫記		77
I-chou ming-hua lu 益州名畫錄		S.3
I-chüeh pien 一角編		56
I-ku-t'ang t'i-pa 儀顧堂題跋		92
Jang-li-kuan kuo-yen lu 穰梨館過眼錄		93
Jung-t'ai chi 容臺集		39
Jung-t'ai pieh-chi 容臺別集		39
Kao Wen-k'o Kung shu hua chen ying mu 高文恪公書畫真贗目, see Chiang-ts'un shu hua mu		
Keng-tzu hsiao-hsia chi 庚子銷夏記		46
Ku-ch'i t'i-pa 姑溪題跋		6
Ku-fen-ko shu hua chi 古芬閣書畫記		88
Ku-kung i-i shu hua mu chiao-chu 故宮已佚書畫目校註		S.21
Ku-kung i-i shu-chi shu hua mu-lu ssu-chung 故宮已佚書籍書畫目錄四種		S.18
Ku-kung shu hua lu 故宮書畫錄		S.22

Ku-yüan ts'ui-lu	古緣萃錄	95
K'uai-yü-t'ang t'i-pa	快雨堂題跋	70
Kuang-ch'uan hua pa	廣川畫跋	7
Kuo-ch'ao yüan hua lu	國朝院畫錄	73
Kuo-yün-lou shu hua chi	過雲樓書畫記	90
Li-tai chu-lu hua mu	歷代著錄畫目	Preface
Li-tai ming-hua chi	歷代名畫記	S.2
Liang-ch'ao ming-hua mu	梁朝名畫目	S.4
Liu-yen-chai erh-pi	六硯齋二筆	38
Liu-yen-chai pi-chi	六硯齋筆記	38
Liu-yen-chai san-pi	六硯齋三筆	38
"Lu-kuo Ta-chang-kung-chu t'u-hua chi"	魯國大長公主圖畫記	17
Lu-yün-lou shu hua chi	麓雲樓書畫記	104
Mai-wang-kuan shu mu	脉望館書目	31
Meng-yüan shu hua lu	夢園書畫錄	87
"Ming-hsin chüeh-p'in"	銘心絕品	10
Mo-yüan hui-kuan	墨緣彙觀	57
Nan-hsün-tien t'u-hsiang k'ao	南薰殿圖像考	59c
Nan-hsün-tien tsun-ts'ang t'u-hsiang mu	南薰殿尊藏圖像目	60
Nan-Sung kuan-ko lu	南宋館閣錄	11
Nan-Sung kuan-ko hsü-lu	南宋館閣續錄	11
Nan-Sung yüan hua lu	南宋院畫錄	55

Nan-t'ien hua pa	南田畫跋	48
Nan-yang ming-hua piao	南陽名畫表	32, 33
Nei-wu-pu ku-wu ch'en-lieh-so shu hua mu-lu	內務部古物陳列所書畫目錄	105
Ni ku lu	妮古錄	43
Ou-po-lo-shih shu hua kuo-mu k'ao	甌鉢羅室書畫過目考	94
Pao hui lu	寶繪錄	41
Pao-yü-ko shu hua lu	寶迂閣書畫錄	101
P'ei-wen-chai shu hua p'u	佩文齋書畫譜	51
Pen-ch'ao ming-hua p'ing	本朝名畫評	
see Sheng-ch'ao ming-hua p'ing		
Pi-hsiao-hsüan shu hua lu	筆嘯軒書畫錄	78
Pi-ko hua mu	秘閣畫目	11
Pi-tien chu-lin	秘殿珠林	58a
Pi-tien chu-lin hsü-pien	秘殿珠林續編	58b
Pi-tien chu-lin san-pien	秘殿珠林三編	58c
Pieh-hsia-chai shu hua lu	別下齋書畫錄	83
P'ing-chin-kuan chien-ts'ang shu hua chi	平津館鑑藏書畫記	79
P'ing-sheng chuang kuan	平生壯觀	S.12
P'u hua chi yü	曝畫紀餘	108
P'u-shu-t'ing shu hua pa	曝書亭書畫跋	53
San-ch'iu-ko shu hua lu	三秋閣書畫錄	107

San-wan liu-ch'ien ch'ing hu-chung hua ch'uan lu 三萬六千頃湖中畫船錄		S.13
San-yü-t'ang shu hua mu 三虞堂書畫目		S.19
Shan-hu mu-nan 珊瑚木難		18
Shan-hu-wang hua lu 珊瑚網畫錄		44
Shang-yen su-hsin lu 賞延素心錄		56
Sheng-ch'ao ming-hua p'ing 聖朝名畫評		3
Sheng-ching ku-kung shu hua lu 盛京故宮書畫錄		100
Shih-ch'ü pao-chi 石渠寶笈		59a
Shih-ch'ü pao-chi hsü-pien 石渠寶笈續編		59b
Shih-ch'ü pao-chi san-pien 石渠寶笈三編		59c
Shih-ch'ü pao-chi san-pien mu-lu 石渠寶笈三編目錄		S.14
Shih-ch'ü sui-pi 石渠隨筆		68
Shih-ku-t'ang shu hua hui-k'ao 式古堂書畫彙考		47
Shih-men t'i-pa 石門題跋		8
Shih-pai-chai shu hua lu 十百齋書畫錄		69
Shu hua chi 書畫記		S.11
Shu hua chien wen piao 書畫見聞表		35
Shu hua chien-ying 書畫鑑影		86
"Shu hua ming-hsin lu 書畫銘心錄"		24
Shu hua mu-lu 書畫目錄		S.6
Shu hua pa pa 書畫跋跋		29

Shu hua shu-lu chieh-t'i 書畫書錄解題	Preface
Shu hua shu-lu chieh-t'i pu chia-pien 書畫書錄解題補甲編	11
Shui-hsin t'i-pa 水心題跋	14
Ssu ch'ao pao hui lu 四朝寶繪錄	
see Pao hui lu	
Ssu-k'u ch'üan-shu 四庫全書	1, S.11
Ssu-k'u ch'üan-shu chien-ming mu-lu 四庫全書簡明目錄	S.11
Ssu-k'u ch'üan-shu tsung-mu t'i-yao 四庫全書總目提要	1, S.11
Ssu-pu tsung-lu i-shu pien 四部叢書藝術編	Preface
Sung-ch'ao ming-hua p'ing 宋朝名畫評	
see Sheng-ch'ao ming-hua p'ing	
Sung Chung-hsing-kuan-ko ch'u-ts'ang shu mu 宋中興館閣儲藏書目	11
Sung Chung-hsing-kuan-ko ch'u-ts'ang t'u-hua chi 宋中興館閣儲藏圖畫記	11
Ta-kuan lu 大觀錄	54
T'ang-ch'ao ming-hua lu 唐朝名畫錄	S.1
Te-yü-chai hua-p'in 德隅齋畫品	S.5
T'ieh-wang shan-hu 鐵網珊瑚 (16 chüan)	30
T'ieh-wang shan-hu 鐵網珊瑚 (20 chüan)	63

T'ien-shui ping-shan lu	天水冰山錄	23
T'ing-fan-lou shu hua chi	聽颿樓書畫記	S.15
T'u-hua chien-wen chih	圖畫見聞誌	2
T'u hua ching-i shih	圖畫精意識	64
T'u-hui pao chien	圖繪寶鑑	S.9
T'ui-an so-ts'ang chin-shih shu hua pa 退盦所藏金石書畫跋		81
Tung Hua-t'ing shu hua lu	董華亭書畫錄	71
Tung-t'u hsüan-lan pien	東圖玄覽編	28
Tzu-i-yüeh-chai shu hua lu	自怡悅齋書畫錄	76
Wang Feng-ch'ang chi	王奉常集	27
Wang Feng-ch'ang shu hua t'i-pa 王奉常書畫題跋		97
"Wang Shih-chen Erh-ya-lou so-ts'ang ming-hua 王世貞爾雅樓所藏名畫"		26
"Wang Shih-mou Tan-pu hua p'in 王世懋澹圃畫品"		27
Wei-kung t'i-pa	魏公題跋	5
Wu-chün tan-ch'ing chih	吳郡丹青志	S.10
Wu-i-yu-i-chai lun-hua shih 無益有益齋論畫詩		96
Wu-lin chang-ku	武林掌故	11
Wu-tai ming-hua pu-i	五代名畫補遺	S.4
Wu-Yüeh so-chien shu hua lu	吳越所見書畫錄	66

Yen-chou-shan-jen kao	弇州山人稿	25, 26, 29
Yen-chou-shan-jen hsü-kao	弇州山人續稿	25
Yen-fu pien	眼福編	91
"Yen shih shu hua chi	嚴氏書畫記 "	22
Yü-chi-shan-fang hua wai-lu	玉几山房畫外錄	62
Yü-i pien	寓意編	19
Yü shih shu hua t'i-pa chi	郁氏書畫題跋記	42
Yü-yü-t'ang shu hua chi	玉雨堂書畫記	84
Yüeh-hsüeh-lou shu hua lu	嶽雪樓書畫錄	85
Yüeh-sheng pieh-lu	悅生別錄	S.7
Yüeh-sheng so-ts'ang shu hua pieh-lu	悅生所藏書畫別錄	S.7
Yün-yen kuo-yen hsü-lu	雲烟過眼續錄	16
Yün-yen kuo-yen lu	雲烟過眼錄	15

MICHIGAN PAPERS IN CHINESE STUDIES

No. 1, *The Chinese Economy, 1912-1949*, by Albert Feuerwerker.

No. 2, *The Cultural Revolution: 1967 in Review*, four essays by Michel Oksenberg, Carl Riskin, Robert Scalapino, and Ezra Vogel.

No. 3, *Two Studies in Chinese Literature*: "One Aspect of Form in the Arias of Yüan Opera" by Dale Johnson; and "Hsü K'o's Huang Shan Travel Diaries" translated by Li Chi, with an introduction, commentary, notes, and bibliography by Chun-shu Chang.

No. 4, *Early Communist China: Two Studies*: "The Fut'ien Incident" by Ronald Suleski; and "Agrarian Reform in Kwangtung, 1950-1953" by Daniel Bays.

No. 5, *The Chinese Economy, ca. 1870-1911*, by Albert Feuerwerker.

No. 6, *Chinese Paintings in Chinese Publication, 1956-1968: An Annotated Bibliography and An Index to the Paintings*, by E. J. Laing.

No. 7, *The Treaty Ports and China's Modernization: What Went Wrong?* by Rhoads Murphey.

No. 8, *Two Twelfth Century Texts on Chinese Painting*, "Shan-shui ch'un-ch'üan chi" by Han Cho, and chapters nine and ten of "Hua-chi" by Teng Ch'un, translated by Robert J. Maeda.

No. 9, *The Economy of Communist China, 1949-1969*, by Chu-yuan Cheng.

No. 10, *Educated Youth and the Cultural Revolution in China*, by Martin Singer.

No. 11, *Premodern China: A Bibliographical Introduction*, by Chun-shu Chang.

No. 12, *Two Studies on Ming History*, by Charles O. Hucker.

(continued)

No. 13, <u>Nineteenth Century China: Five Imperialist Perspectives</u>, selected by Dilip Basu, edited with an introduction by Rhoads Murphey.

No. 14, <u>Modern China, 1840-1972: An Introduction to Sources and Research Aids</u>, by Andrew J. Nathan.

No. 15, <u>Women in China: Studies in Social Change and Feminism</u>, edited with an introduction by Marilyn B. Young.

No. 16, <u>An Annotated Bibliography of Chinese Painting Catalogues and Related Texts</u>, by Hin-cheung Lovell.

Price: $3.00 (US) each,
except $3.50 for special issues #6 and #15

* * *

MICHIGAN ABSTRACTS OF CHINESE AND
JAPANESE WORKS ON CHINESE HISTORY

No. 1, <u>The Ming Tribute Grain System</u> by Hoshi Ayao, translated by Mark Elvin.

No. 2, <u>Commerce and Society in Sung China</u> by Shiba Yoshinobu, translated by Mark Elvin.

No. 3, <u>Transport in Transition: The Evolution of Traditional Shipping in China</u>, translations by Andrew Watson.

Price: $3.50 (US) each

* * *

Michigan Papers and Abstracts available from:
Center for Chinese Studies
University of Michigan
Lane Hall
Ann Arbor, Michigan 48104 USA

www.ingramcontent.com/pod-product-compliance
Lightning Source LLC
Chambersburg PA
CBHW032133040426
42449CB00005B/227